Companion to t
Revised Common Le

3. All Age Worship Year B

Already published

Companion to the Revised Common Lectionary

1: Intercessions

2: All Age Worship Year A

Judy Jarvis and Donald Pickard

Companion to the Revised Common Lectionary

3. All Age Worship Year B

EPWORTH PRESS

Permission of the copyright holder to use the extract on p. 9
from Dom Helder Camara, *It's Midnight Lord*, Pastoral Press 1984,
is gratefully acknowledged.

0 7162 0530 0

*First Published 1999
by Epworth Press
20 Ivatt Way
Peterborough, PE3 7PG*

*Typeset by Regent Typesetting, London
Printed and bound in Great Britain by
Biddles Ltd, Guildford and King's Lynn*

Contents

Contributors

Alan Amos
Clare Amos
Judy Davies
Ian Haile
Eric Jarvis
Judy Jarvis (Editor)
Andrew Lunn
Julie Lunn
Stephen Mosedale
Ruth Parry
Donald Pickard (Editor)

The editors wish to express their thanks
not only to all the contributors but in particular to
Mary Roseweir for all her work and support

Introduction

> 'Whom is worship for?'. The answer is, 'Worship is for God'. Worship is offered to God by God's people. The congregation is not the audience, but the cast ... (Neil Dixon, *Epworth Review*, 1993).

These words reflect a conviction which underpins this volume of the Companion to the Revised Common Lectionary. It has been prepared in order to encourage all people, whatever their experience, background or age, to share together in offering worship to God.

Worship involves our whole being. With this in mind this book offers a variety of opportunities for exploration and discovery, for inter-action and for liturgical action in order to encourage the offering of our whole selves. For example, for most Sundays there is a suggestion for a worship centre to be a visual focus for prayer, meditation and action. Also contained within the text are ideas which draw on all the senses as well as drama, meditation, choral speaking and dance. In the appendices, along with some supplementary information, are listed songs which can be used in different ways as part of worship.

Producing this book has been a group process. As writers we have met on a number of occasions. Together we decided how to approach the challenge which faced us, shared our material, listened and made suggestions. We have learnt a great deal from the process and from each other.

All the prayers and meditations are firmly based on the readings for the Principal Service for Year B of the Revised Common Lectionary. For the Sundays in Ordinary Time in the second half of the year, the lessons are laid out on three lines. On the top line are the 'semi-continuous' Old Testament readings: on the second line are the alternative, 'related' readings. The Epistle and Gospel on the third line are the same for either set of Old Testament readings. Within the constraints of space we could not give the same emphasis to all the readings. Other material based on the readings can be found in the first book in this current series, *Intercessions*. We have, however, given a heading for each Sunday, which may offer a common thread to link together thoughts, images and prayers, and to provide shape and coherence in planning acts of worship. We are well aware that our 'common threads' may be different from those perceived by others. We offer them as ideas, as starting points for shared preparation.

The 'full, conscious and active participation of all the people' which is one of the watchwords of the renewal of worship in our times implies using language which is accessible to the whole church community. With this in mind we have tried to communicate through images which are stimulating and creative, but not too obscure, and to employ ideas and symbols which are original and imaginative but also grounded in everyday experience.

> Worship is a celebration in which all present recall and rejoice in the mighty acts of God. It is ... a party, in honour of the divine guest, at which members of the family, young and old, have something and someone to celebrate. (Neil Dixon, ibid.).

We invite you to join in.

Judy Jarvis and Donald Pickard

ALL AGE WORSHIP YEAR B

Advent Liturgy

This liturgy can be built up during Advent, but can be restricted to one sentence and one response each week. The song 'Christmas is Coming' is suggested here, but others, such as the hymn 'The Holly and the Ivy', may be used instead.

The Advent Ring

Use a traditional Advent ring of four coloured candles and a central white candle or create an advent ring, as follows:

Week 1	Provide an 'oasis' ring (available in different sizes from florists). Ask volunteers from the congregation to bring forward pieces of evergreen and to place them in the ring. (Use something that will last well, e.g. conifer.) Put one red candle in place.
Week 2	Members of the congregation add more evergreen material (e.g. holly) and a second red candle.
Week 3	Members of the congregation add further evergreen material or wired fir cones and a third red candle.
Week 4	Members of the congregation add further evergreen material or red silk poinsettias and a fourth red candle.
Christmas Day	Members of the congregation add fresh white carnations and place a larger white candle in the centre of the advent ring.

Lighting the Advent Candles

Advent 1

Restore us O God, let your face shine that we may be saved (*Psalm 80.3*)

Come to us as light for our world.
Come to us O God. (*The first candle is lit*)
Song 'Christmas is Coming' (Chorus, first verse, chorus)

Advent 2

The grass withers, the flower fades, but the word of our God will stand for ever. (*Isaiah 40.8*)

Come to us in the words of your prophets.
Come to us O God. (*Two candles are lit*)
Song 'Christmas is Coming' (Two verses and choruses)

Advent 3

There was a man sent from God whose name was John. He came as a witness to testify to the Light, so that all may believe through him. (*John 1.6–7*)

Come to us through your witness John.
Come to us O God. (*Three candles are lit*)
Song 'Christmas is Coming' (Three verses and choruses)

Advent 4

My soul tells out the greatness of the Lord. My spirit has rejoiced in God my Saviour. (*Luke 1.46–47*)

Come to us in the joy of Mary.
Come to us O God. (*Four candles are lit*)
Song 'Christmas is Coming' (Four verses and choruses)

Christmas Day

And the Word became Flesh and lived among us, and we have seen his glory, the glory as of the Father's only Son, full of grace and truth. (*John 1.14*)

Christ is come. Alleluia.
Christ is come. Alleluia! (*All the candles are lit*)
Song 'Christmas is Coming' (Whole song)

FIRST SUNDAY OF ADVENT

Isaiah 64.1–9; Psalm 80.1–7, 7–19; I Corinthians 1.3–9;
Mark 13.24–37.

ACTIVE WAITING

Worship Centre *A piece of clay and a clay pot should be placed where everyone can see them.*

Opening Sentence (*Mark 13.37*)
Jesus said to his disciples, 'And what I say to you, I say to everyone: keep awake.'

Advent Liturgy
Use the Advent Liturgy (see pp.2–3).

Confession
Lord, we have not kept watch for you.
We have occupied ourselves with our own concerns.
We have not waited to find your will for us.
We have not noticed the needs of the people around us.
We have not acknowledged the love that has been shown to us.

Forgive us for our lack of watchfulness.
Help us to wait to know your will.
Help us to look out for the needs of others.
Help us to work and watch for your coming.

'I am making all things new' says the Lord

This is Christ's gracious word:
'Your sins are forgiven.'

Amen. Thanks be to God.

Meditation
Someone holds up the ball of clay during the first part of the reading.

A   Clay – heavy, smooth, solid, dark,
        deep in the earth,
        dug from the soil,
        wrenched from the ground.

B   Clay – heavy, smooth, solid, dark,
           thrown on the wheel,
           spun into shape,
           handled with love.

The clay is replaced and the clay pot is raised.

C   The potter – the maker, the creator,
           handling the clay,
           shaping the clay,
           moulding the clay.

Both clay and pot are raised.

D   God the potter,
           We are clay made by your hands, You formed us, urging us
           into life, but handling us with care and love.

A,B,C and D (and/or the congregation)
           We, the clay,
           place ourselves in your hands: our joys and our sorrows, our
           fears and our failures.
           We, the clay,
           place ourselves in your hands: for re-shaping and re-newal,
           for re-moulding and re-use.
           We, the clay,
           offer ourselves to you, seeking your Advent hope.

Dismissal (*I Corinthians 1.3 and 9*)
    Grace and peace to you from God our Father and the Lord Jesus
    Christ. It is God himself who called you to share in the life of his
    Son, Jesus Christ our Lord; and God keeps faith. **Amen.**

SECOND SUNDAY OF ADVENT

Isaiah 40.1–11; Psalm 85.1–2, 8–13; 2 Peter 3.8–15; Mark 1.1–8.

MAKING A PATH FOR GOD'S COMING

Worship Focus *Before the act of worship place stones on a path though the building e.g. starting from the foundation stone/church porch ... font – lectern – communion table ... moving out from the church.*

Opening Sentence (*Isaiah 40.3*)
A voice cries out:
'In the wilderness prepare the way of the Lord,
make straight in the desert a highway for our God.'

Advent Liturgy
   Use the Advent Liturgy (see pp. 2–3).

Prayer of Approach
God, you came to your people in the past.
Through the wilderness, you guided them;
When they were lost, you searched for them;
When they were in exile, you brought them back home.
   For your love which stays close: **We praise you, God.**

God, you come to your people now.
In our worship, you speak to us;
In our journey through life, you go with us;
When we look for a way, we see it in Jesus.
   For your love which calls us to follow: **We praise you, God.**

God, you will come to your people in the future.
When times are uncertain, your promises remain;
Your kingdom will come, on earth as in heaven;
Your whole creation will be made new.
   For your love which holds us forever: **We praise you, God.**

Confession (*based on Isaiah 40.3–4*)
During the confession members of the congregation gather the stones from the path into a basket.

Lord, sometimes we block your way of love.
   Clear a path: **Prepare the way of the Lord.**

6

When we are selfish and thoughtless;
when we hurt others by what we say and do;
forgive us.
    Clear a path: **Prepare the way of the Lord.**

When we are timid and fearful;
when we shrink from the challenge of following you;
forgive us.
    Clear a path: **Prepare the way of the Lord.**

When we are divided from one another;
when we are so sure that we are right
that we stop listening to those who think differently;
forgive us.
    Clear a path: **Prepare the way of the Lord.**

The basket of stones is brought up to the table.

Lord, we come to you as we are.
Forgive the things in us which resist your love.
Help us to be your people, preparing your way.
Amen.

Prayer of Response (*from II Peter 3.13*)

Faithful God,
We trust in your promise
that one day your kingdom will come.

We pray for those who suffer unjustly ...
God of justice, we look for a world where justice is at home.

We pray for those who are anxious ...
God of peace, we look for a world where peace is at home.

We pray for those who feel unloved ...
God of love, we look for a world where love is at home.

God of justice, peace and love,
may your kingdom come;
and may it be seen in us,
as we live for you day by day,
through Christ our Lord. **Amen.**

THIRD SUNDAY OF ADVENT

Isaiah 61.1–4, 8–11; Psalm 126 or Canticle: Magnificat;
I Thessalonians 5.16–24; John 1.6–8, 19–28.

PREPARING FOR THE LIGHT

Worship Centre *Place, alongside the advent ring, an unlit candle
and matches, an oil lamp and oil, a large torch and batteries, a table
lamp with an extension lead.*

Opening Sentence (*I Thessalonians 5.24a*)
The One who calls you is faithful.

Advent Liturgy
Use the Advent Liturgy (see pp.2–3).

Prayer of Praise *(based on Isaiah 61.1-4, 8-11)*
God, you are a wonderful God!
You take care of those whose hearts are broken,
You give great comfort to those who mourn.
Let us rejoice in the Lord. **Let us exult in our God.**
You bring good news to those who think they are worthless,
You help those who feel imprisoned to break free.
Let us rejoice in the Lord. **Let us exult in our God.**
You love justice and hate all that is wrong,
Your promise lasts for ever.
Let us rejoice in the Lord. **Let us exult in our God.**

Ministry of the Word
*Talk about preparations, both for the Christmas general festivities
and for the coming of Jesus as Light of the world. Ask different
people to prepare and light the lights in the worship centre. Use the
following prayer.*

Prayer for the Lighting of the Lights
John came into the wilderness –
Not just a wilderness of stones and barren places,
But a wilderness of wrong, shortsightedness and selfishness,
A wilderness of people not knowing the way to go.
He came to tell of the Light –
He came to tell of the Light.

John comes into our wilderness –
Not just a wilderness of frantic life and shattered dreams,
But a wilderness of wrong, short-sightedness and selfishness,
A wilderness of people not knowing the way to go.
He comes to tell of the Light –
He comes to tell of the Light.

John comes to bring news of the Light –
Not just a light to brighten the dark and barren places,
But a light to re-kindle hope, to set us on fire,
A beacon for people not knowing the way to go.
He comes to bring us Light –
He comes to bring us Light

Reflection
The spirit is breathing.

All those with eyes to see,
women and men with ears for hearing
detect a coming dawn;
a reason to go on.

They seem small, these signs of dawn,
perhaps ridiculous.

All those with eyes to see,
women and men with ears for hearing
uncover in the night
a certain gleam of light;
they see the reason to go on.
Dom Helder Camara

Dismissal Prayer *(based on I Thessalonians 5.16–24)*
Go in peace: aim at what is best for each other,
  always be joyful,
  pray continually,
  give thanks, whatever happens.
And may God, the God of peace,
make you holy through and through
and keep you sound in spirit, soul and body.
The grace of our Lord Jesus Christ be with you.

FOURTH SUNDAY OF ADVENT

II Samuel 7.1–11, 16; Psalm 89. 1–4, 19–26
or Canticle: Magnificat; Romans 16.25–27; Luke 1.26–38.

HOW GOD'S PROMISES ARE FULFILLED

Worship Centre *Prepare a 'shrine' – four rectangular sides with a flat square on top. Cover the pieces with a wood effect ('a house of cedar') or with gold paper. There is also a large display board, for the five pieces of the 'shrine' to be set out, during the readings, in the shape of a cross.*

Opening Sentence (*Romans 16.25, 27*)
Rejoice! for God has revealed the divine secret, kept in silence for long ages. To God be the glory for ever!

Advent liturgy
Use the Advent Liturgy (see pp. 2–3).

Prayer of Approach
God of mystery, whom no eye has seen, you are yourself for us a sign. Set within our hearts your living Word, so that we may proclaim your presence, God with us, in Jesus Christ. **Amen.**

Ministry of the Word
A   The prophet Nathan looked for an everlasting kingdom of David's family.
'I will make you a great name among the great ones of the earth. Your kingdom shall stand for all time.'
Surely, this was God's promise: yet it was not to be.
Read II Samuel 7.1–11, 16.
Your spirit and power, O God, cannot be confined.
You are mighty in all the earth!
Sing a hymn or a carol: place the top part of the 'shrine' in the centre of the board.
B   Down the ages, the people longed for the One whom God would send, a King in the line of David.
'For a boy has been born for us, a son given to us. And he shall be called in purpose wonderful, in battle God-like, Father for all time, Prince of Peace.'
Surely, this was God's promise: yet it was not to be.
Read Romans 16.25–27.
Your spirit and power, O God, cannot be confined.
You are mighty in all the earth!

Sing a hymn or a carol: place a wall of the 'shrine' on each side of the piece in the centre of the board.

C   So the people of God looked for a King, and the peoples of the nations for a Prince of Peace. When the time was right, God's messenger came to a young woman.

'The Holy Spirit will come upon you, and the power of the Most High will overshadow you.'

Mary of Nazareth was dreaming of God's Kingdom: surely, this is how God's promises come to be. But God is not to be confined by our expectations: God's way has to be traced from the bare manger to the bitter cross.

Read Luke 1.26–35.

Your spirit and power, O God, cannot be confined.

You are mighty in all the earth!

Sing a hymn or a carol: place the remaining walls of the 'shrine' above and below the central piece, to form a cross.

Praise and Acclamation

Listen to a recording of a setting of the Magnificat. Use the following responses and then listen to the music again.

Tell out, tell out the greatness of the Lord!

Amen, Lord! You are holy, you are mighty!

Rejoice, rejoice in God our Saviour!

Amen God! Your ways are wonderful!

God has scattered the proud, turning their dreams to nightmares!

Yes Lord! We know your power!

God takes care of the humble, and brings their dreams to life!

Let it be, Lord! Let the gentle inherit the earth!

God fills the earth with promise, so the hungry will be fed!

That's the way for it to be! Let us share our bread today!

God's love is never-failing: sure from age to age!

Amen! From beginning to end, you are God!

Dismissal Invitation

Let us go, in heart and mind, to see what has come to pass:

Let us go with the shepherds:

Let us go to find the Saviour!

Let us go with the wise ones:

Let us go to find God's promise, born for us!

Let us go with the poor and humble:

Theirs is the Kingdom of God!

Let us go with all the world: with all the peoples of the nations:

Come, let us worship, come, let us adore him: **Christ the Lord!**

CHRISTMAS DAY

Isaiah 52.7–10; Psalm 98; Hebrews 1.1–4 (5–12); John 1.1–14.

COSMIC CHILD

Worship Centre *A crib.*

Prayer of Praise (*suggested by Psalm 98.7–8*)
*Sung responses to use after each section could be the chorus of
'See amid the winter's snow', or the South African chant 'Amen
Siakudumisa!'*

The oceans shout aloud for baby Jesus,
the fish leap and the whales sing;
and one day ... all will be silent
when he says, 'Be still'.

The mountains roar for this tiny Jesus.
Reaching up to the sky, they cry for joy;
and one day ... they will be silent
when he walks in light upon them.

The sea sings to the child Jesus,
its waves roar and surf hisses on the beach;
and one day ... they will rejoice again
when he walks upon them.

The hills shout for infant Jesus
for he comes to judge the earth;
and one day ... they will be heavy
with his burden.

Meditation
*At the end of each of the following sections a symbol is placed near
the crib.*
God of light, what have you started,
bringing this child into the world?
Even as we long for it, we are frightened of that light,
because it might show us up, and we would be ashamed.
But how can we be frightened of a baby?
May we welcome his light, and know your love.
A powerful torch or searchlight is placed near the crib.
Baby Jesus, smaller than we are,
you are higher than the angels.

God of fairness, what have you started,
bringing this child into the world?
We want our world to be a fairer place,
but we do not want to give up our privilege, our presents,
all we are so lucky to have.
Yet this child is giving us everything,
and do we need more than him?
May we embrace his justice, and accept his judgment.
A pair of scales is placed near the crib.
Baby Jesus, smaller than we are,
you are higher than the angels.

God of all the world, what have you started,
bringing this child into the world?
Our world is such a big place,
and we struggle to see beyond our own worries.
But this little infant reaches out to the ends of the earth.
May the whole world see him, know him, and shout for joy.
A globe is placed near the crib.
Baby Jesus, smaller than we are,
you are higher than the angels.

Offertory Prayer
Blessed are you, Lord God of all creation.
Out of your love and goodness alone, you spoke in the beginning.
From your Word all things came to be,
and without him nothing came into being.
Without him we would have nothing to give.

In the beginning was the Word:
we offer you our word and our words.
In him was life:
we offer our lives.
In his life was light for all people:
we open ourselves to the light.
The light shines on in the darkness:
and the darkness cannot put it out.

Dismissal
God-is-with-us: Go in peace to love and serve the Lord.

FIRST SUNDAY OF CHRISTMAS

Isaiah 61.10–62.3; Psalm 148; Galatians 4.4–7;
Luke 2.15–21, 22–40.

WAITING REWARDED

Opening Sentences (*Isaiah 62.1–3*)
Three wrapped presents lie on a small table. They contain: a candle, stand and matches; a nativity figure of Jesus; a crown or wreath of flowers. As they are unwrapped they are left on the table, perhaps standing on their wrapping paper.
For Zion's sake I will not keep silent, and for Jerusalem's sake I will not rest,
until her vindication shines out like the dawn, and her salvation like a burning torch.
> *The candle is unwrapped and lit.*

The nations shall see your vindication, and the kings your glory;
and you shall be called by a new name that the mouth of the Lord will give.
> *The Christ figure is unwrapped.*

You shall be a crown of beauty in the hand of the Lord,
and a royal diadem in the hand of your God.
> *The crown/wreath of flowers is unwrapped.*

Dramatic Presentation
The participants face in different directions, ignoring each other.
A is reverent and formal: B is casual, almost off-hand.
A The waiting is over.
B Christmas is over, at last.
A The gift has been presented.
B The wrapping paper's all in the bin, and some of the presents are already broken.
A And what will we do with it now?
B Not too much of the turkey left to eat.

A Simeon has waited for him through all the long years.
B At least the children will get over their excitement now.
A Such patience he has shown in his worship and his waiting.
B They really were the limit the last few days before Christmas.
A For him this is the moment which will change the world.
B Really over the top.
A Now he can go in peace, to sleep the final sleep of an old man.
B Bit of peace and quiet at last.

14

A And Jesus lies before us,
   with all the promise of his life in front of him.
B Just sit back and enjoy the telly now.
A Simeon speaks of the future, with words to chill Mary's heart.
B Wouldn't you know it: two good films tonight at the same time.
A '... and a sword will pierce your own soul too'.
B Won't have time to watch it all anyway, I suppose.
A The waiting is over, and yet it has only just begun.
B Have to video some of it for later in the year.

A When Anna sees him, she praises God.
B The January sales start tomorrow.
A She cannot keep silence, because her waiting is rewarded.
B Must try to get in early tomorrow, before the queues get long.
A She speaks about the child to everyone,
B I must be mad:
   shopping before Christmas, shopping after Christmas ...
A because now he is here, can the world ever be the same again?
B Ah well, not long before it's all over for another year.
A So the waiting is over.

Prayer of Praise and Dismissal
Response to be sung at the beginning and after each section.

Jesus, we have been waiting for you. And now you have come
bringing light for all the nations of the world;
bringing glory to those among whom you have chosen to live.

Jesus, we have been waiting for you. And now you have come
to turn the world upside down;
to bring down the mighty and raise up the weak.

Jesus, we have been waiting for you. And now you have come
as a Word spoken in our heart;
as a Word which cannot stay silent within us, but must be shared.

Jesus, we have been waiting for you. And now you have come
to send us out in peace, for our waiting is over;
to send us out in joy, because a new day has dawned.

SECOND SUNDAY OF CHRISTMAS

Jeremiah 31.7–14; Psalm 147.1–20 or Sirach 24.1–12 or Wisdom of
Solomon 10.15–21; Ephesians 1.3–14; John 1.(1–9)10–18.

HIDDEN THINGS REVEALED

Worship Centre *A parcel, in Christmas wrapping, to be used for
the activity.*

Prayer of Praise
God of mystery, Creator, forever eternal,
It was you, it was you
from before the beginning,
deciding and planning, making and blessing,
God of mystery revealed
We praise you now.

God of mystery, lover, encourager,
It was you, it was you
bringing your people home
comforting, refreshing, restoring, forgiving,
God of mystery revealed
We praise you now.

God of mystery, queenly Wisdom,
It was you, it was you
Spirit of life, authoress of vision
inspiring, stirring, leading your people,
God of mystery revealed
We praise you now.

God of mystery, Word incarnate,
It was you, it was you
the eternal in time
teaching, healing, awakening your people,
God of mystery revealed
We praise you now.

Activity
Play a game of pass the parcel.
*Between each of the layers are verses from the Bible to be read
aloud.*
Suggested verses from today's readings:

16

Fatherhood (Jeremiah 31.9 – part); shepherd (Jeremiah 31.10b); healer (Psalm 147.3–4); Wisdom (Sirach 24.1a, 3–4); God's choice of us in Christ (Ephesians 1.4); God's secret purpose (Ephesians 1.9a, 10b); John sent to testify to the light (John 1.6–7).
In the centre of the parcel there is a model of Jesus in the manger which is placed on the worship centre; the reading is John 1.1–4.

Declaration of Faith
John 1.15b 'This is the man of whom I said, "He comes after me, but ranks ahead of me," before I was born, he already was.'

This is the man, his name is Jesus
the one we follow, our brother and friend
born in poverty, living in simplicity
to show us the wealth of God's life without end.

This is the man, his name is Jesus
the one we follow, our brother and friend
a man for the people, teaching and healing
offering his people life without end.

This is the man, his name is Jesus
the one we follow, our brother and friend
Word from the beginning, creating and shaping
and in us making his life without end.

This is the man, his name is Jesus
the one we follow, our brother and friend
glory of God, eternal truth telling
revealing God's grace for life without end.

This is the man, his name is Jesus
the one we follow, our brother and friend
this is the man, our God revealing
to bring us to the Father, to life without end.

Dismissal
'The Word has become flesh, and lives among us.'
Go in peace to love and serve the Lord.

EPIPHANY

Isaiah 60.1–6; Psalm 72.(1–9)10–15; Ephesians 3.1–12;
Matthew 2.1–12.

GOD FOR EVERYONE

Worship Centre *A large cake and three crowns from crackers
placed on a table laid with party cloth.*

Prayer of Praise
God, you have made yourself known,
but in a most amazing way,
coming in weakness, in a tiny baby ,
you covered your glory and hid your greatness.
God of mystery and surprise we praise you.

God, you have made yourself known,
but in a most amazing way,
in a dirty poor stable no one else wanted;
you hid your wealth and infinite riches.
God of mystery and surprise we praise you.

God, you have made yourself known,
but in a most amazing way,
born to humble working people,
hidden in a simple life,
and yet announced in the stars of heaven and visited by kings.
God of mystery and surprise we praise you.

Sharing the Epiphany Cake
*Traditionally an iced fruit cake (decorated with stars, crowns, angels,
flowers and the three kings) was shared at Epiphany.*
*Share the cake beginning with a child, spreading out gradually
through the congregation as the following piece is read, by one,
two or several voices. This action should follow the reading from
Ephesians with its emphasis on the gospel being for all, illustrating
the widening out and inclusive nature of the gospel. Alternative –
Galette des Rois (see Appendix 1).*
The gospel of God is known in a child,
a tiny child, a helpless child.
The gospel of God embraces two parents,
caring and loving the tiny child.

The gospel of God is proclaimed to some shepherds,
faithful and listening,
who drop what they're doing to worship the child.
The gospel of God reaches out to the Magi,
far, far away, watching and learning, who see the star
and travel a long time with gifts for the child.
The gospel of God is taught to fishermen,
ordinary fisherman by the sea,
who abandon their nets to follow the child.
The gospel of God is preached to crowds,
old men, young women, children who gathered,
wanting to hear and receive from the child.
The gospel of God is revealed on a cross, the gospel in action,
for centurion and governor, for enemy and friend
who were stunned by the love of the child.
The gospel of God is proclaimed in resurrection,
wonderful joy for frightened and faithful, doubtful and trusting,
all who saw God in the child.
The gospel of God goes out through the frightened ones,
now all transformed,
telling the story the wide world over, to all who will listen,
and know God in the child.
The gospel of God is now here among us, between us and in us,
is here now for all of us, and all of God's people, in all time and
space; for all who find God in the child.

Dismissal Prayers
Through the brightness of a star, O God,
you unfolded the mystery of salvation to all the nations.
In Christ, and through the preaching of the gospel,
draw the ends of the earth into one family
so that all the world may give you glory.
We ask this through Jesus, your Son,
Who is Immanuel, God-with-us. **Amen.**

God of Advent, of waiting and hoping,
keep our hearts expectant, ready for your coming among us.
God of Christmas, of celebration and rejoicing,
make our hearts glad with the joy nothing can take from us.
God of Epiphany, of hiding and making known,
fill our hearts with wonder at the revelation of your glory we have
seen in Christ our Lord. **Amen.**

SUNDAY BETWEEN 7 AND 13 JANUARY

First Sunday in Ordinary Time

Genesis 1.1–5; Psalm 29; Acts 19.1–7; Mark 1.4–11.

THE VOICE OF GOD

Worship Centre *A jumble of large-piece jigsaw puzzles on a central table. People should be invited to come during the service to do the puzzles, so that by the end they are complete.*

Call to Worship
In the beginning ... God.
From chaos ... form.
From darkness ... light.
From silence ... a word.
In our confusion, busyness, noise ... God's word in us.
In our beginning ... God.

Prayer **A Meditation on a Jigsaw Puzzle** — *Opening with God, creator*
Lord, sometimes life is like a jigsaw puzzle, *close with Christ our*
higgledy-piggledy pieces in a heap, *redeemer.*
all confused, nothing fitting together.
Each piece is different: some are plain blue reflecting serenity,
others a riot of colour, a bit of this, a bit of that,
expressing vitality perhaps, chaos maybe.
Sometimes we try to sort the pieces out a bit,
find the corners, separate the straight edges,
begin to piece the picture together.
But sometimes,
just when we think we can see the picture which is our life,
it doesn't make sense... *we remain confused, even afraid.*
But you, Lord, remember the emerging picture.
You do not forget.
You wait with us in our confusion
and when the time is right,
gently prompt us to pick up the spilt pieces and go on.
So speak order out of chaos once again.
Show us where we can find the corner pieces of ourselves
and the straight edges
and with your deft and gentle touch
make the puzzle with us, bit by bit,
until your time is right, and we are complete.

20

And thank you that there is both delight in putting together a puzzle
and in seeing it finished.

Meditation
*This meditation, following the Gospel, is largely silent, allowing
space for reflection after each phrase. (Up to two minutes each time
is possible, but needs careful introduction.)*

Listen for the word of God. God speaks to you, to me, to us all,
today.   *Silence*
God says, 'You are my beloved.'   *Silence*
God says, 'I have chosen you.'   *Silence*
God says, 'My favour rests upon you.'   *Silence*
This is the word of the Lord.
Thanks be to God

Song *To link the Meditation and the Prayer*
'Be still, for the presence of the Lord'

Prayer of Petition *(for two voices)*
A   From silence, a word.
      In the silent chaos of depression and disorder, which longs for
      serenity and stillness,
B   Voice of God command your comfort and peace.
A   In the silent wasteland of despair and fear, which longs for
      reassurance and hope,
B   Voice of God whisper your comfort and peace.
A   In the silent desert of loneliness and grief, which longs for
      comfort and a human touch,
B   Voice of God speak your soothing word of comfort and peace.

B   From noise, silence.
      In the noisy busyness of television or chatter which shields us
      from ourselves,
A   Silence of God resound your stillness and peace.
B   In the noisy wordiness of worship which prevents us from
      hearing you,
A   Silence of God echo your stillness and peace.
B   In the noise of frenetic activity which gives us no time to think
      and no time for you,
A   Silence of God breathe your Spirit of stillness and peace.

SUNDAY BETWEEN 14 AND 20 JANUARY   Second Sunday in Ordinary Time

I Samuel 3.1–10 (11–20), Psalm 139.1–6, 13–18;
I Corinthians 6.12–20; John 1.43–51.

DISCERNING GOD

Opening prayer
'God be in my head.'
Sing or read with pauses between the phrases.

Litany   *To follow the scripture readings*

A   You know me God: teach me to know you.
       You have found me God: teach me to find you.

B   In the temple of my body, in the depths of my being

A   In my thoughts and my words, in the deeds of my hands
       Teach me to find you.

B   You call me and call me.

A   Speak Lord,
       your servant is listening.

B   You know me God: teach me to know you.
       You have found me God: teach me to find you

A   In the highways and byways of city and village
       On park bench, under fig tree, in stranger and neighbour.

B   You call me and call me
       Come and see
       Find me.

A   Rabbi,

A&B You are the Son of God;
       The king of Israel.

Spiritual Exercise

This exercise will need time. Each person should have two colours of pencil/pens and paper. Make sure that those who would like, including younger children, have large sheets of paper and access to a range of coloured pens, which will provide them with opportunity to show special events of their lives in pictures. It is important that people are given enough time to think quietly at each stage. Since this activity is to help individuals, people will not be expected to share what they do with others, though children may wish to do so.

Draw a horizontal line on your paper. This line represents your life so far, beginning at the left hand end with your birth. Mark on the line any significant points in your life history – birth of siblings, deaths, achievements, special events etc.

In a different colour mark on the line occasions when you have been particularly aware of God's presence.

Spend time silently pondering how your awareness of the presence of God relates to your life experiences. What happens at the 'low' times? At the 'high' times? Are there times when you have not been aware of God at all for long periods? Why might that be? How do you expect God to make himself known to you? Looking back, has God made himself known in ways you do not normally expect?

Finish by reading Psalm 139.1–6, 13–18.

Prayer of Dedication
either
This is my body, a holy place for you God.
I have a heart to love with your love
a mind to think your thoughts
feet to stand firmly on your way
hands to create and caress
eyes to look at our sisters and brothers with compassion
ears to hear your laughter and your cries of pain.
I have a body here Lord
a body you made and gave
your holy place
for me
and for the world. **Amen.**

or
This is my body, a holy place for you, God:
a body for love with passion and purity
a body for caring with gentleness and empathy
a body for acting with determination and intent
a body for prayer in silence and emptiness
a body for you God, restless Lover,
tireless peace-maker,
for you whose Word spoke the world into being
for you whose silence fills every void
for you God, for whom the Universe is a holy place.
This is my body,
a holy place for you. **Amen.**

SUNDAY BETWEEN 21 AND 27
JANUARY   Third Sunday in Ordinary Time

Jonah 3.1–5, 10; Psalm 62.5–12; 1 Corinthians 7.29–31;
Mark 1.14–20.

TIME TO TURN

Worship Centre *A large clock, placed centrally which, if possible,
can be made to chime eleven to symbolize the eleventh hour.*

Call to Worship
Time is short. **Christ have mercy.**
We are called to repent. **Christ have mercy.**
The right time has come. **Let us hear good news.**
God is very near. **Spirit of Life, move among us.**
    Clock chimes (or use a chime bar)

Call to Repentance
'The time is fulfilled, and the Kingdom of God has come near;
repent, and believe in the good news.'

There is no better time than now:
to turn away from complacency,
which says we do not need to change;
to turn away from greed,
which grasps more and more for ourselves;
to turn away from self-centredness,
which blots out what others need.
Now, today, we are sorry for all we have done wrong.

There is no better time than now:
to turn towards hope, which says that tomorrow belongs to God;
to turn towards trust, as we put ourselves in God's hands;
to turn towards compassion and towards our neighbour.
Now, today, we want to live better lives.
    Pause
This is the good news.
Jesus has come. Today he says to us: 'You are forgiven.'
Amen. We can begin again. Thanks be to God.

Meditation (*based on I Corinthians 7.29–31*)
*This meditation should follow the reading. Read slowly with long
silences between paragraphs. Conclude with a piece of quiet music.*

24

Think of a time when you had to make up your mind.
A serious decision with serious consequences.
And you did not have all the time in the world:
your decision was wanted, waited for. It is the eleventh hour.
Think of a time when you had to make up your mind.

So many things come into your head to clutter up your thinking.
Concerns about your family, your future,
or what someone else would think.
You cannot tell all these things to go away.
They are the things which matter to you,
which make you who you are:
you are someone who mourns, or rejoices, or worries;
you are someone who deals with the world.
Remember the concerns which fill your mind.

But to make your decision,
you must weigh these heavy, precious things.
You weigh lives in your hands: your life, and the lives of others.
Wouldn't it help if you could put these things down,
precious as they are?
Put them down with someone you can trust: with God?
Wouldn't it help to step back from them, and look again.
Imagine yourself doing that now.
Let yourself be like someone who deals with the world,
but who becomes as though they had no dealings with it.

The appointed time has grown short.
Now is the time to make your decision.
Now, while your concerns are in God's care.
Afterwards you can take them up again; reclaim them.
But will they ever be so precious again,
now you have put God in front of them?
How does it feel now to make your decision?

Act of Dedication
Jesus said, 'Follow me and I will make you fish for people.'

When people are desperate: **may we bring them to safety.**
When they are lonely: **may we give friendship.**
When they are sad: **may we bring them to Jesus.**

Friends of Jesus, he calls you today.
May we follow him from now until the end of our days.

SUNDAY BETWEEN 28 JANUARY AND 3 FEBRUARY
Fourth Sunday in Ordinary Time

Deuteronomy 18.15–20; Psalm 111; I Corinthians 8.1–13;
Mark 1.21–28.

CONFRONTING EVIL

Prayer of Confession
Lord, when we have spoken,
we have not always spoken with your love,
but have hurt others by what we have said.
Lord, have mercy. **Christ, have mercy. Lord, have mercy.**
Lord, when we say we are doing what you want,
we are not always truthful,
but please ourselves instead of following you.
Lord, have mercy. **Christ, have mercy. Lord, have mercy.**
Lord, when your people speak,
we do not always speak on your authority,
but say what we want to hear, or what feels more comfortable.
Lord, have mercy. **Christ, have mercy. Lord, have mercy.**
Lord, when your church speaks,
we do not always speak with your love,
but injure your body with our prejudice and pride.
Lord, have mercy. **Christ, have mercy. Lord, have mercy.**
Silence
Lord, when you speak,
we can trust your words completely;
when you talk, we cannot but listen;
when you challenge us, we hear of God's love;
and we are glad when we hear you say to us,
'Your sins are forgiven.' **Amen. Thanks be to God.**

Prayer of Praise
Holy God, stronger than evil, **Your praise endures for ever.**
Good God, we remember your wonderful deeds:
overcoming chaos to make a world so ordered and intricate,
from atom to star, your pattern is stamped on creation.
Holy God, stronger than evil, **Your praise endures for ever.**
Good God, we remember your wonderful deeds:
setting your enslaved people free, and making them your own,
bringing them home, when they were lured away.
Holy God, stronger than evil, **Your praise endures for ever.**

26

Good God, we remember your wonderful deeds:
facing down Satan in the desert, and expelling his followers,
stilling the storm and quieting the sea.
Holy God, stronger than evil, **Your praise endures for ever.**
Good God, we remember your wonderful deeds:
sharing our pain through Jesus,
embracing our death through Jesus,
in Jesus entering death's deep shadow,
from which you raised him up.
Holy God, stronger than evil, **Your praise endures for ever.**
Good God, we remember your wonderful deeds:
washing away our divisions with the flood of your Spirit,
consuming our prejudice with your fire of judgment.
Holy God, stronger than evil, **Your praise endures for ever.**
Good God, we remember your wonderful deeds.
We are your people, you are our God.
As you stand against evil, may we stand with you.
Holy God, stronger than evil, **Your praise endures for ever.**

Blessing before Preaching
Blessed are you, God of all creation.
You spoke in the beginning, and all things came to be.
You spoke, and your Word came to live with us,
full of grace and truth.
Bless this place where we would hear your voice.
Bless this place where we would hear your story.
As we listen, may our ears be attuned to you.
As the word is spoken, may you speak to us.
May all we hear lead us to you.

Confronting Evil
From the Mark reading prayers could focus on the need to root out
evil. Ask the congregation to talk to each other about evils they are
aware of in our contemporary world. Leave a pause for reflection
then say the following prayer.
Holy God, stronger than evil:
in the name of Jesus, and by the power of the Spirit,
root out from our lives and from our world
all that twists your truth and misuses your power.
Deliver us from evil; command it to come out.
Silence
The Lord's Prayer.

SUNDAY BETWEEN 4 AND 10

FEBRUARY Fifth Sunday in Ordinary Time

Isaiah 40.21–31; Psalm 147.1–11, 20c; I Corinthians 9.16–23;
Mark 1.2–39.

INFINITE CREATOR, INTIMATE GUEST

Worship Centre/Activity *A table with many shiny silver paper stars, cut out beforehand or during the service. Two voices start counting softly, alternating numbers, 'One, two, three, four ...'. The call to worship is spoken over the 'numbering'. At various points in worship the 'numbering' is heard, using bigger and bigger numbers e.g. 304; 305; 306; ... etc. At the very end of the service the 'numbering' which by this stage should be vast acts as a backdrop to the dismissal and gradually fades away.*

Call to Worship (*Psalm 147.3-5*)
The Lord heals the brokenhearted: **and binds up their wounds.**
The Lord numbers the stars one by one: **and calls each by name.**
Mighty is our Lord and great is his power !

Prayer of Approach
Lord, you are the creator of the myriad of stars,
yet at the same time you come to us as our intimate guest.
As we wonder at the glory of your creation,
we find your presence has crept into our lives.
Heal our brokenness with your tender love,
And through our weakness bring strength to others:
May our spirits soar on eagles' wings,
bearing the news of your kingdom to earth's furthest bounds,
to the glory of your name. **Amen.**

Prayer of Adoration (*based on Isaiah 40.21–31*)
Congregation A: **Have you not known?**
Congregation B: **Have you not heard?**
1: Count the shining stars of heaven.
2: How can we? There are so many!
1: Are they not all the signs of God's work?
2: Does God not reach out through all of space?
   Whom can we compare with God?
Congregation A: **Have you not known?**
Congregation B: **Have you not heard?**

1: Dream the dreams of earth's creation.
2: How can we? It was all so long ago!
1: The foundations of time, are they not held in God's hands?
2: Is God so old? Is God so young?
   Whom can we compare with God?
Congregation A: **Have you not known?**
Congregation B: **Have you not heard?**
1: Listen to the voices of the weary and downcast.
2: How can we? They're not loud enough for us to hear!
1: Yet the whispers of the brokenhearted speak to God's heart.
2: Is God so near? Is God even *within*?
   Whom can we compare with God?
Congregation: **Have we not known, have we not heard?**
              The Lord who created us calls us by name!

Prayer of Thanksgiving and Intercession
Ask people to write on the stars the names of those they wish to pray
for. Stick them on a dark background in patterns representing famous
constellations.

Infinite God we give you thanks:
We thank you for those who face danger,
inspiring others by their courage:
Lord, in your mercy: **Hear our prayer.**

Infinite God we give you thanks:
We thank you for those who care for creation :
Lord, in your mercy: **Hear our prayer.**

Intimate God we give you thanks:
We thank you for friends and families,
we praise you that you have made each one of us so different;
help us to respect others for their differences from ourselves,
so that together our gifts may be brought into the harmony of your
    kingdom.
We thank you for those whom we have loved but see no longer,
and pray that, with them, we may share in the shining joys of
    heaven.
These prayers we ask in the name of Jesus Christ. **Amen.**

Dismissal and Blessing
May the Lord of the stars of light bless you with his light,
May Jesus, the hope of the world, kindle in you his steadfast love,
and may the Holy Spirit, who gives the breath of life,
renew your strength, now and always. **Amen.**

SUNDAY BETWEEN 11 AND 17
FEBRUARY   Sixth Sunday in Ordinary Time

II Kings 5.1–14; Psalm 30; I Corinthians 9.24–27; Mark 1.40–45.

CO-OPERATING WITH GOD THE HEALER

Worship Centre *A bundle of rags, representing both the clothes of people with leprosy and their bandages.*

Call to Worship
In the name of God who creates us and heals us
We bring our thanks and praise.

Prayer of Approach (*based on Psalm 30.5, 11–12*)
Lord of life's movement,
you can turn our weeping into dancing;
Weaver of life's pattern,
you can strip off our sackcloth, and clothe us with joy.
Weeping may linger for a night, but joy comes in the morning.
O Lord, our God, we will give thanks to you for ever.

Reflection *Questions for discussion following the reading of the Gospel (NB: Mark 1.41 has been translated 'moved with anger' and 'moved with pity').*
Pity or anger?
With what or with whom might Jesus have been angry?
How does the idea of anger fit with our picture of Jesus?
Are we brave enough to accept that sometimes anger is called for?
What might be modern parallels to the situation that Jesus had to
    confront?

Meditation
Use fabric pens to write on the rags words that express how the world treats 'outsiders', ie those who metaphorically wear rags. With deliberation, bin the rags: offer the following meditation:
If I should boast of being clean and whole, my Lord
then shall I be found filthy, diseased and in rags;
If I should flaunt myself as a leader among your servants
then shall I stumble in among the last to obey your call;
If I should pride myself on a life of discipline and obedience
then I may hear your voice saying, 'Friend, do you love me?'
But if I give my strength in the service of others, I shall find you;

If I look for you in prison, or among the dying, I shall find you there;
And if for love of you I turn aside from my own choosing, then
I shall find myself among your chosen ones
at the coming of your kingdom.

Prayers of Intercession and Offering
The response could be sung to an Orthodox chant (see p.124).
Remember your servants, Lord, when you come into your kingdom.

We pray for those who seek healing of mind and body,
for patients in local hospitals, and for their doctors and nurses.
Remember your servants, Lord ...
We pray today especially for people with leprosy,
and for those who seek to cure them,
giving thanks for the struggle to eradicate this disease.
Remember your servants, Lord ...
We pray for all persons living with HIV and AIDS,
conscious of its impact on the developing world,
and the families and friends who mourn their loved ones.
Remember your servants, Lord ...
We pray for those whose lives have been changed by illness:
for those who stand alongside, offering costly support,
and for those who work in campaigning agencies, in hospices and
community homes
Remember your servants, Lord ...
We pray for those who exploit others in society, and who need to
change their ways:
for drug dealers, for bad employers, for heartless landlords,
Help your church confront them with the challenge of the gospel.
Remember your servants, Lord ...
We pray for ourselves:
that we may be ready to respond with passion and commitment.
Give us eyes to see where you look for healing, and the courage to
answer your call.
Remember your servants, Lord ...

Dismissal and Blessing
May Christ be your healing and your comfort,
Christ your strength in adversity,
and Christ your friend in every danger,
and may the kiss of God, the Spirit given from the Father,
be with you and surround you this day and always. **Amen.**

SUNDAY BETWEEN 18 AND 24 FEBRUARY

FEBRUARY Seventh Sunday in Ordinary Time

Isaiah 43.18–25; Psalm 41; II Corinthians 1.18–22; Mark 2.1–12.

YES TO GOD

Worship Centre *A rolled mat, representing a bed mat and/or a sleeping bag or camp bed.*

Call to Worship (*based on Isaiah 43.18–19*)
Do not keep on about the 'good old days':
Stop saying 'We have always done it this way.'
Our God is doing a new thing!
It's happening now: can you not see?

Prayer of Approach
Lord God, we come to you knowing that you will hear us,
We thank you that you are close to us, and care for us.
You are not a God who is far away;
You travel with us, and you understand us.
We thank you and we praise you,
because in Jesus Christ you share in our lives
and make your love known. **Amen.**

Meditation (*for two voices, to follow the reading of the Gospel*)
A The past is comfortable.
  I feel so secure there.
  No, I don't want to move. No, I don't want to change.
B But God is doing for you a new thing,
  do you not see the way he has made for you?
A Let me stay behind.
  Freedom is too frightening. I want to say No.

A I'm not a bad person,
  just afraid to be forgiven now.
  No, I don't want God's risky challenge.
  No, it is too costly to stand up and be restored.
B But Jesus offers you acceptance
  pledges to you the 'Yes' of his own life.
A If only my friends would carry me,
  resting me gently in your presence
  I might begin to say 'Perhaps'.

A The future is being formed,
   I am invited into it.
   Am I brave enough to trust God's faithfulness,
   to offer my assent to his love?
B In the community of the faithful you will find a welcome.
   Those around you will uphold you, giving their Amen.
A I will allow Christ to set his seal on me,
   I am free to declare God's praise,
   I will say 'Yes' for evermore.
Pause for reflection

Activity
Ask everyone turn to their neighbour in the congregation, and offer a sign of peace saying: '(X), your sins are forgiven for Jesus' sake.' The other person responds 'Amen, Thanks be to God' – and in turn offers this sign of peace and forgiveness to another person, so that everyone is included.

Prayer of Thanksgiving
Lord, we thank you for our friends who help us at times
when we cannot seem to help ourselves.
We thank you for those who help us
by telling us the truth as they see it,
even when we do not wish to hear it.
We give you thanks: **And praise your holy name.**

We thank you for those in our society who care for others ...
(e.g. for those whose employment involves caring: ambulance drivers, health personnel, firefighters ... or other occupations represented in the congregation and for those involved in caring in other ways: volunteers and visitors, or carers, who are often unrecognized or unacknowledged).
We give you thanks: **And praise your holy name.**

We thank you for the opportunities for service which you give us.
Open our eyes, that we may see your will for us,
and be ready to do it.
We give you thanks: **And praise your holy name.**

Dismissal
May God go with you as you share the good news of the Kingdom:
Amen.
May Christ meet you in friend and stranger: **Amen.**
May the Spirit uphold you and be your guide: **Amen.**

SUNDAY BETWEEN 25 AND 29 FEBRUARY Eighth Sunday in Ordinary Time

or THE SUNDAY BETWEEN 24 AND 28 MAY (if after Trinity Sunday)

Hosea 2.14–20; Psalm 103.1–13, 22; II Corinthians 3.1–6; Mark 2.13–22.

THE PASSION OF GOD'S LOVE FOR US

Worship Centre *A small table on which are piles of envelopes (see the final activity with the dismissal).*

Call to Worship (*based on II Corinthians 3.2–3*)
(Paul writes) 'You yourselves are our letter, written on our hearts, to be known and read by all.'
Show that you are a letter of Christ,
written not with ink but with the Spirit of the Living God.

Prayer of Approach
God of all faithfulness,
you have opened the gate of mercy for your people
and are always ready to welcome those who turn to you.
Look on us in your compassion,
that we may gladly respond to your love
and faithfully walk in your way
through Jesus Christ our Lord. **Amen.**

Activity
Use the symbol of the (wedding) ring as a basis for discussion. Have a large 'ring' painted on a flipchart or shown on an overhead projector to represent the circle of Christ's love. Ask people to make suggestions to be included in this circle. Is there anything we would wish to put outside the circle? Draw a cross through and beyond the circle, to make the shape of a Celtic cross.

Bidding Prayers
Response (based on Hosea 2.15):
L: Turn our valleys of troubling: **R: Into gateways of hope.**
We pray for all who seek a new beginning in their lives ...
– for those who know stress and conflict in their workplace ...

- for those who have sought employment without success ...
- for those who know prosperity, but seek something more ...
- for those who have made sacrifices for the sake of others ...
- for those who care for the sick in their homes ...
- for those who know the pain of broken relationships ...

Prayer of Offering
Jesus, our lover,
we pledge ourselves to you.
Excite us with your cherishing,
empower us with your passion,
that we may know you more intimately,
and faithfully honour our troth of righteousness and mercy.
Speak tenderly to our hearts saying: I will be your God:
And we shall be your people.

Jesus, physician of the soul,
we come to you for healing.
Challenge us with your daring,
and restore us through your wounds of love,
that we may embrace the way of the forsaken,
and bleed alongside your rejected ones.
Speak tenderly to our hearts saying: I will be your God:
And we shall be your people.

Jesus, foretaste of God's new wine,
we drink deep from your life-giving spirit.
Intoxicate us with your love,
quench our longing with your refreshing coolness,
that we may burst the skins of easy convention
and drench the world with profligate compassion.
Speak tenderly to our hearts saying: I will be your God:
And we shall be your people.

Dismissal
*Give out the envelopes from the worship centre. Each envelope
should contain a Memo with the following words:* Show that you are
a letter of Christ, written not with ink but with the Spirit of the living
God (II Corinthians 3.3). *Ask everyone to open their envelope and to
read it (helping each other as necessary) before the final prayer:*
Let us go in the peace of Christ, the Beloved,
serving him with love and tenderness among our neighbours,
so that we all may know him in our hearts
as steadfastly as we ourselves have always been known. **Amen.**

SUNDAY BEFORE LENT

II Kings 2.1–12; Psalm 50.1–6; II Corinthians 4.3–6; Mark 9.2–9.

LISTEN AND SEE

Worship Centre *Three candles, one of which is taller.*

Call to Worship
Solo voice 'Be still and know that I am God' (v. 1).
Silence
The candles are lit by three people from around the congregation.
All sing 'Be still and know that I am God'
Be still and know that I am God, says the Lord.
Let the mountains quake before the presence of the Shining One.
Let light shine out of darkness:
The glory of God shines in Jesus' face.

Prayer of Approach
Hush now! Listen, be silent
For the Word of creation has leapt down in the quiet of night.
Hush now! Listen, be silent
For a still, small voice echoes in heavenly chariots of fire.
Hush now! Listen, be silent
The Son speaks on the mountain to disciples tongue-tied with awe.
Hush now! Listen, be silent
Glory shines on the face of the crucified one, wordless in death.

Look now, listen and wonder
God's word is a burning fire.
Look now, see and wonder
The place where you stand is holy.
Turn aside, look now and wonder
At the brightness of eternity that awaits you.
At the whisper of God that echoes in you.
Silence
Be still and know that I am God, says the Lord.
Let light shine out of darkness:
The glory of God shines in Jesus' face.

Prayer of Adoration
Holy God
Mysterious name: **In your light, we shall see light.**
Hidden name: **In your light, we shall see light.**
Powerful name: **In your light, we shall see light.**

Sorrowful name: **In your light, we shall see light.**
Loving name: **In your light, we shall see light.**
Holy Name: **In your light, we shall see light.**
Beautiful name: **In your light, we shall see light.**
Compassionate name: **In your light, we shall see light.**
Silence
Be still and know that I am God, says the Lord.
Let light shine out of darkness:
The glory of God shines in Jesus' face.

Confession
Forgive us, God.
We allow your gospel to be muffled and refuse to hear,
We allow your word to deafen us, and refuse to listen,
Open our ears that we may hear.
We allow your light to blind us, and refuse to see,
We allow your gospel to be hidden, and refuse to search,
Open our eyes that we may see.

God of light and love,
Help us to know and believe
that we may walk in the light of your Son, Jesus Christ our Lord.
Amen.

Prayer of Commitment
Help us, dear Lord,
Build your house –
Like Moses, in truth and justice,
Like Elijah, speaking forth your word,
Like your Son, with liberating love –
Three in One,
Build us thus, dear Lord:
Your word, the Law written,
Your word, the prophets spoke,
Your word, your Son revealed,
Your word, may my life be. **Amen.**

Prayer at Dismissal *(standing at the worship centre)*
Lord Jesus, may your face shine upon us
Like the bright sun ...
Warmth to give, Light to guide,
Life to live – Lives transfigured
Lives transformed.
May God bless us and keep us, and give us peace. **Amen.**

FIRST SUNDAY IN LENT

Genesis 9.8–17; Psalm 25.1–10; I Peter 3.18–22; Mark 1.9–15.

GOD'S COVENANT WITH EVERY LIVING CREATURE

Worship Centre *Place the font at a focal point. If it is a small font, place it on a table covered by a drape in 'rainbow' colours or use narrow strips of crepe paper to create a rainbow.*

Call to Worship (*Genesis 9.13*)
God said,
> My bow I set in the clouds
> to be a sign of the covenant
> between myself and the earth.

Prayer of Approach
Lord our Creator, you gave us our world, and all that is in it:
> all birds and flying creatures,
> all fish and swimming things,
> all people, made to be like you.

Lord our Sustainer, you have given us your promise:
> that you will always be near to us, our children and our children's children,
> that all living creatures are in your care,
> and that your promise is for ever. **Amen.**

Meditation/Reflection
The reader stands at the worship centre.
Water is poured into the font
> Water is life

> Cool, clear water,
> Water to quench our thirst.

> Fresh flowing water,
> Water to make things grow.

> Pulsing, thrusting water,
> Water to bring us power.

> Water is life.
Water is poured into the font

Water is death

Brown polluted water,
Causing disease.

Flooding, frightening water,
Bringing destruction.

Scarce, precious water,
Drying up, failing.

Water is death
Water is poured into the font

Waters of death and life,
God's living water.
Waters of new hope and joy
Baptism through death to life.
Water is poured into the font

Prayer of Thanksgiving (*based on Psalm 25*)
Loving God,
We thank you for your faithfulness,
In you we put our hope.
We thank you for your tender care,
In you we put our hope.
We thank you for your unfailing love,
In you we put our hope.
We thank you for your goodness,
In you we put our hope.
Teach us your ways,
In you we put our hope.

Dismissal and Blessing
Loving God:
Help us during this time of Lent to stay with you.
Help us not just to hear your word but to trust your promises.
Lord have mercy
Help us to repent, to believe the gospel, and to recognize your
kingdom with us.
Lord have mercy.
May God who calls us in baptism, go with us on our journey of
faith; and the blessing of God ...

SECOND SUNDAY IN LENT

Genesis 17.1–7, 15–16; Psalm 22.23–31; Romans 4.13–25;
Mark 8.31–38.

FOLLOWING JESUS: THE WAY OF THE CROSS

Entrance Procession *Carry a cross in a procession into the church during the singing of a hymn, e.g. 'Lift high the cross', 'Majesty', or 'The royal banners forward go'.*
Stop between the verses of the hymn to read Bible verses tracing the way to the cross:

Luke 3.22	Mark 1.39	
Mark 10.32	John 12.32	End with Mark 8.34

Prayer of Approach
Covenant God
You promise to be with us, you call us to be for you.
We come to worship you:
we want to praise your name.
Help us to be ready to follow, wherever you lead us
And to give you praise, this day and every day.
We pray in Jesus' name. **Amen.**

Prayer of Confession (*the response may be sung as a 'Kyrie'*)
God, our God,
Is your way our way now,
in this world, so in need of your mercy and your grace?
Have mercy!
> **Lord, have mercy!**
We hear many voices:
Which shall we follow?
Have mercy!
> **Lord, have mercy!**
God, our God
Dare we follow you?
Are we ready to count the cost of the way to the cross?
Have mercy!
> **Lord, have mercy!**
Faithful God,
Help us to accept your forgiveness and renew us by your Spirit
that we may follow in the way of Jesus, our Saviour. **Amen.**

Gospel Activity
Ask a child to start a game for everyone of 'Simon says' (in which everybody does the action if it is prefaced by 'Simon says' but not otherwise), as an introduction to the idea of 'Follow my leader'.

Litany
Servant Christ, help us to follow you into the waters of baptism
to link our lives with all those grieved about injustice and wrong:
to be renewed by your Spirit, to bring good news to the poor
and to set free the oppressed ...
Help us to follow you:
Help us to follow you, Christ the Servant.
Servant Christ, help us to follow you in ministry:
to heal and restore the broken body of humanity
to intercede for those in need ...
Help us to follow you:
Help us to follow you, Christ the Servant.
Servant Christ, help us to follow you on the way to Jerusalem:
to claim the life of city, town and village for God, whose image we
    bear,
to confront those who rely on power for oppression
with the startling message of your love in action.
Help us to follow you:
Help us to follow you, Christ the Servant.
    (Based on *The Litany of Christ the Servant*, Bangalore)

At the Offering
Give everyone a piece of paper in the shape of a cross
Invite people to write (with pencil or in 'finger-writing') on each arm of the cross a focus for prayer:
    a family member or close friend
    a person in the church or local community
    a situation in their home country
    a situation in the news
In the centre, each person traces his or her own name.
As an act of offering, the crosses are brought forward (either individually or all together) and placed at the foot of the processional cross.

Blessing
May God who goes before us strengthen us for our journey:
and the blessing of God ...

THIRD SUNDAY IN LENT

Exodus 20.1–17; Psalm 19; I Corinthians 1.18–25; John 2.13–22.

THE WISDOM OF GOD

Worship Centre *Place where it can be seen a very large stone to represent a tablet of stone on which the Ten Commandments were written. Near to it place a small table, covered with a cloth. On the table put large piles of coins.*

Call to Worship *(Psalm 19.7–8)*
The law of the Lord is perfect and revives the soul.
The precepts of the Lord are right and give joy to the heart.
The commandment of the Lord is pure and gives light to the eyes.

Prayer of Approach
Covenant God,
You have been with us throughout history.
You made the world and all that is in it.
The wonder of your creation is all around us.
You are the Lord our God:
    We praise your name for ever.

You brought your people to freedom,
You make us free through your love.
You are the Lord our God:
    We praise your name for ever.

You made it known that you, and you alone, were God.
As the one God, we worship you.
You are the Lord our God:
    We praise your name for ever.

You gave your people a pattern to live by.
Help us to rediscover a pattern in our lives.
You are the Lord our God:
    We praise your name for ever.

Invite everyone to stand. Read the Ten Commandments (Exodus 20), standing beside the stone which represents the tablets of stone on which they were received.
Hear the commandments which God has given to his people:
– I am the Lord your God: you shall have no other God besides me.
– You shall not idolize anything God has made.

- You shall not dishonour the name of the Lord your God.
- Remember the Lord's Day and keep it holy.

Lord have mercy on us:
and turn our hearts to delight in your law.

- Honour your father and your mother
- You shall not murder
- You shall not commit adultery
- You shall not steal
- You shall not give false evidence
- You shall not set your hearts on anything which is your neighbour's

Lord have mercy on us:
and turn our hearts to delight in your law.

Meditation/Reflection *(for two voices)*

A   It was time to worship,
        It was time to remember,
        It was time for the festival.

B   Jesus set his face towards Jerusalem.

A   In the temple there was buying and selling,
        In the temple there was bickering and arguing,
        In the temple there was cheating and lying.

B   Jesus went into the temple.
        Out of the temple he drove the animals,
        Out of the temple the birds flew free,
        Out of the temple he threw the moneychangers.

Pull the cloth from under the coins, scattering them as far as possible.

Prayer of Dedication

Wise and loving God,
We recognize that your foolishness is wiser than our wisdom,
We acknowledge that your weakness is greater than our power,
We know that you choose us, in our foolishness and weakness.
You call us to understand and proclaim a message which is
    offensive to some and nonsense to others.
Be with us in our foolishness,
Be with us in our weakness,
In your strength, make us wise and strong. **Amen.**

Blessing

May God who challenges us in Jesus enable us to follow:
and the blessing of God ...

FOURTH SUNDAY IN LENT

Numbers 21.4–9; Psalm 107.1–3, 17–22; Ephesians 2.1–10; John 3. 14–21.

THE LOVE OF GOD MAKES US ALIVE
(for further suggestions see also Mothering Sunday, pp.122–23)

Worship Centre *Have a wide variety of things placed together on a table including inanimate objects: e.g. a stone, a torch, a watch, a book, a glass of water, a teddy bear – and some symbols, like badges, and animate objects, a leaf, a plant, an animal (e.g. a fish or a hamster). Include among the objects a robot toy of some kind, preferably one that simulates human characteristics.*

Call to Worship *(Psalm 107.1)*
Give thanks to the Lord, for he is good; his love endures for ever.

Prayer of Approach
Loving God, we worship and adore you.
Your love for us never ends.
You sent Jesus into the world
showing us how to live,
showing us how to be fully human.
Even though we did not understand
and turned against him,
you still love us.
We praise you because you made this world to be our home.
We praise you because you are with us wherever we go.
We praise you that you made us able to think, and speak and love.
Loving God, we worship and adore you because your love for us
    never ends. **Amen**

Confession
Forgive us God our creator
that we have not always lived as you would want.
When good things happen we forget you,
when bad things happen we blame you.
    Loving God, **forgive us.**

Forgive us God our creator
that our care for others is often inadequate.
When we are self-centred and heartless,

and we do not help others to become whole,
Loving God, **forgive us.**

Forgive us God our creator
that we turn away from your love,
When we ask you to guide us but go our own way,
and when we think we can order you to do what **we** want,
Loving God, **forgive us.**

God hears us and forgives us,
set us free from wrong and strengthens us to do right.
In love, we are accepted.
We belong to God.   **Thanks be to God. Amen.**

Ministry of the Word
Standing by the worship centre, begin with a question like:
What's the difference between a stone and a plant?
Use the objects on the worship centre to explore what it means to be alive and human. After introductory discussion focus on the robot toy (or if one is not available, refer to this category of object). Using the toy, talk about robots which have human characteristics. Lead into an exploration of the comparison between being human and being a robot, with the following questions:
What are the advantages of being a robot?
What are the advantages of being human?
The important things to emphasize are the things which make us distinctively human. Following this ask one or two people to talk about what it means to them to believe and follow Jesus.

Meditation
In love God made the world.
In love God sent the Son *(pause)*
not to condemn us, but to save us. *(pause)*
In love God saved us.

We are saved by the love of God,
by the Son, sent in love. *(pause)*
Believe in him. *(pause)*
Live in him. *(pause)*
God is love.

Blessing
May God who loves the world bring us to eternal life:
and the blessing of God ...

FIFTH SUNDAY IN LENT

First Sunday of the Passion

Jeremiah 31.31–34; Psalm 51.1–12 or Psalm 119.9–16;
Hebrews 5.5–10; John 12.20–33.

OUR NEW RELATIONSHIP WITH GOD

Worship Centre *A collection of flower bulbs or onions, if possible with some growth. Have some which are whole and some cut open. A flowering plant grown from a bulb.*

Call to Worship
Jesus said, 'When I am lifted up from the earth I will draw all people to myself.'

Adoration
Loving God,
We come to you in worship and thanksgiving.
You are greater than we can understand;
open our eyes that we may see the wonderful truths
you have shown to us in Jesus.

You are more loving than our hearts can respond to;
help us to give ourselves to you in worship
so that we learn what you want us to be.

You are wiser than we can know;
still our minds as we worship you
so that we can understand the things you are saying to us.

Loving God, in Jesus,
You chose to come to the world in humility.
You chose the path the world saw as foolish.
You used what the world considered weak.
We worship and adore you. **Amen**

Reflection and Meditation
Talk about what the bulbs look like inside. In the very centre of a bulb is the important part that will grow to be the flower, the bit that carries the message relating to what that bulb will produce. The rest is there to feed the growing flower and so is important in that respect and must be cared for. It is the heart of the bulb, the very centre, that bears fruit.

Relate this to the covenant with God being written on the hearts of the people and also to the wheat falling to the ground.

The heart, the centre, the core, beating,
keeping us alive with its regular rhythm.
Sustaining life.

The heart, symbol of love and tenderness, gentle,
making us alive to other people.
Loving life.

The heart, breaking with grief,
aching, sharing in the sorrow of the world.
Living life.

God says, 'I will write my laws on their hearts.'
The heart, a part of God, knowing God.
Living, loving, sustaining for God.

The heart of God, pierced for us,
knowing, loving, forgiving.

Confession and Absolution
Loving God, we know that you love us:
so we confess that we have let you down.
Every day we betray you, deny you, misunderstand you,
    crucify you.
We betray you when we are selfish or unkind.
We deny you when we do not speak out for justice and truth.
We misunderstand you when we justify our actions by misquoting
    your teaching.
We are truly sorry and we wait for your word of love.

Listen to the promise.
God says:
I will be your God and you shall be my people.
I will forgive your sins and put them out of my mind.

Blessing
May God who makes all things new transform our living:
and the blessing of God ...

SIXTH SUNDAY IN LENT

Second Sunday of the Passion/ Palm Sunday

Mark 11.1–11 *or* John 12:12–16; Psalm 118.1–2;
Isaiah 50.4–9a; Psalm 31.9–16; Philippians 2.5–11;
Mark 14.1–15.47 *or* Mark 15.1–39 (40–47).

OBEDIENCE TO GOD

Entrance Procession *Start with a joyful processional hymn. People of all ages enter waving palm branches. Distribute palm leaves to the rest of the congregation.*

Adoration

A 'See your King comes to you, gentle and riding on a donkey.'
B Lord, on this Palm Sunday may we recognize in you
  the one who comes to this world
  and join with full hearts in the cries of Hosanna!

A 'Hosanna to the Son of David!'
B It would have been so easy to bask in this popularity,
  to be deflected from your mission.
  Yet you humbled yourself, living as we live and dying for us.

A 'Blessed is he who comes in the name of the Lord!'
B We give you our praise and love
  for all you have shown to us and done for us. **Amen**.

Activity *(to follow the Gospel reading)*
*This activity links the making of palm crosses to the different stages of the service. Show people of different ages how to make the crosses beforehand in order that they can help others. The instructions can be found in Appendix 1 (p.125). The appropriate step is undertaken at the points indicated *1–9.*

Confession

*Stage 1. Split the palm leaf down the centre to represent brokenness

Loving God,
You rode a donkey and came in peace,
humbled yourself and gave yourself for us.
We confess our lack of humility.

As you entered Jerusalem, the crowds shouted Hosanna:
Save us now!
On Good Friday they shouted Crucify!
We confess our praise is often empty.
We sing Hosanna but cry Crucify

As the crowd laid their palms in front of you
you took the way of God: you took no glory for yourself.
We confess that we want to be accepted and take the easy way.
We do not stay true to your will.

Absolution
Let us make the cross-piece to symbolize Christ surrounding us
with loving forgiveness.
*(Stages *2-4)*
Merciful God, we thank you:
even though we find it so difficult to live according to your will,
your arms are always stretched out to welcome us in loving
     forgiveness.
We ask for your forgiveness and to be made whole.
Hosanna! **Hosanna: set us free!**

Know that you are forgiven: be at peace.
Hosanna! **Hosanna in the highest! Amen.**

Ministry of the Word
*Complete the crosses, helping each other (stages *5-9). This stage
symbolizes that it is by being broken, bent and surrounded by the love
of Christ we allow that love to become a part of us, becoming
complete.*

Read Mark 15.20b–39.
Ask people to hold the crosses while singing one of the following:
     'Jesus remember me, when you come into your kingdom'
     'When I survey the wondrous cross'

Blessing
May God whose arms were spread on the cross to embrace the whole
world help us this week to take up the cross and to follow him:
and the blessing of God ...

EASTER DAY

Acts 10.34–43; Psalm 118.1–2,14–24; I Corinthians 15.1–11;
John 20.1–18.
or Isaiah 25.6–9; Psalm 118.1–2,14–24; Acts 10.34–43;
John 20.1–18 *or* Mark 16.1–8.

RESURRECTION

Worship Centre *Construct a large representation of a tomb some-where in the church, using large stones and turves, or tables draped with white sheets, or painted cardboard boxes. (NB This 'tomb' is also part of the suggestions for the worship centre for the following Sundays of Easter.)*

Approach to Worship
Begin the worship with a dramatic reading of the Gospel.
Either – have the area where the worship centre is as dark as possible. Three women walk slowly towards it, heads down, looking sad and quietly discussing what will happen when they arrive with regard to the stone. As they approach the front a light shines on a figure dressed in white who speaks to them the words of Mark 16.6–7
Or – use the Empty Tomb (John 20.1–18) from The Dramatised Bible.

Call to Worship *(by the person who played Mary Magdalene)*
Alleluia! The Lord is risen! **Alleluia! He is risen indeed!**

Dressing the Tomb
People bring symbols of new life, (e.g. flowers, pot plants, fresh eggs, paper butterflies etc.) during the singing of an extended Alleluia! or the first hymn, and place them round the 'tomb'.

Confession and Absolution
People of God, what did you carry to the cross on the hill?
We brought anger and bitterness,
hurt pride and wounding tongues,
arrogance, mockery and greed.
We carried them to the cross of Christ, to be nailed there.
People of God, what did you carry down to the grave?
We brought frustration and loss, anxiety, fear and despair.
We carried them to the tomb of Christ, to be buried there.
People of God, what are the burdens you carry to the garden tomb?

We bring our guilt and shame for the wounds that we caused.
We carry the emptiness of our faded hopes,
and the hurt of our failure.
Pause
People of God, what do you bring to the empty tomb,
this resurrection morning?
We bring the groanings of our world,
and the hunger of its people,
the vain hopes for peace,
and the frustration of violence and hate.
We carry them, with heavy hearts.
But who will roll away the stone?
Pause
As the dew falls, fresh every morning,
and flowers turn towards the new-born sun:
So God rolls away the burdens of our heavy hearts,
and sets us free to live with Christ.

Jesus says: 'Peace be with you!'
In the name of Jesus Christ, our sins are forgiven!
Amen! Thanks be to God! Alleluia!

Thanksgiving
Blessed are you, God, for this day, for this first day:
on which the story of our making
becomes one with the hope of all things made new.
This is the day of liberation,
when you call us into life through death.

Blessed are you, God, for your call to freedom:
for rolling away the stones that imprison the spirit;
for the women stumbling, in the half-light of the dawn,
into the light of your glory.
You open up the mystery which we celebrate with all your people!
End with a sung 'Alleluia!'

Blessing
Go in peace: the risen Christ goes before you.
Go in joy: the stone is rolled away: the risen Christ goes with you.
Go in love and strength: the risen Christ lives within you. Amen.

SECOND SUNDAY OF EASTER

Acts 4.32–35; Psalm 133; I John 1.1–2.2; John 20.19–31.

THE SHARING COMMUNITY

Worship Centre *If not already in place, construct an empty tomb made from large stones and turf at the beginning of the act of worship.*

Music 'Easter Hymn' from *Cavalleria Rusticana* (Mascagni).

Call to Worship
Alleluia! Christ is risen!
Alleluia! He is risen indeed!
He unites us in heart and soul.
We share joy in his resurrection.
Sung Alleluia *Either* 'Alleluia, the Lord is risen' (see Appendix 1)
or the chorus of 'Good Christians all, rejoice and sing'

Adoration
We worship you, God.
You are the creator.
You bind together this wonderful world.
  You bind us together.
We worship you, God.
Your energy flows through creation.
We marvel at the vastness of the universe.
  You bind us together.
We worship you, God.
You created this world and gave us life.
We thrill to respond to the knowledge that you share it with us.
  You bind us together.
We worship you, God.
We marvel most of all at your love in sending your Son
We celebrate his risen life together.
  You bind us together.

Confession
God who loves us
we seek forgiveness.
You call us to trust that Jesus lives.
Forgive our lack of belief.   **Help us to trust you.**
You call us to trust what we have not heard;
Forgive our lack of belief.   **Help us to trust you.**

52

You call us to trust what we have not seen.
Forgive our lack of belief. **Help us to trust you.**
You call us to trust what we have not touched.
Forgive our lack of belief. **Help us to trust you.**
You call us to trust each other.
Help us to believe despite our unbelief.
Help us to receive your peace. _to live in the joy of_
Help us to be at peace with you and each other. _resurrection promise_

Theme Prayer
God, three in one, unite us today
so that we may share all that we have and are
as the community of the Spirit in the power of the resurrection.

The Peace
The Risen Lord be with you. **And also with you.**
Share the Sign of Peace.
(perhaps using 'The Peace of the Lord', Brian Hoare)

Thanksgiving
God, we thank you that, in creating this universe,
you have given us life.
In freeing us from death, you have given us eternal life.
By your Spirit, you have given us life together.
We thank you for the Christian life we share in this congregation
and with Christians everywhere.
For our life together in Christ: **We thank you, God.**
Thank you that we share the truth about Jesus Christ;
Help us to be honest.
For our life together in Christ: **We thank you, God.**
Thank you that we share the peace of Jesus Christ;
Help us to be sincere.
For our life together in Christ: **We thank you, God.**
Thank you that we share the common life in Jesus Christ;
Help us to be generous.
For our life together in Christ: **We thank you, God.**
Thank you that we share the wonder of the resurrection;
Help us to do so with joy
For our life together in Christ: **We thank you, God.**

Dismissal
The peace and the presence of the Risen Christ be with you;
and the blessing of God ...

THIRD SUNDAY OF EASTER

Acts 3.12–19; Psalm 4; I John 3.1–7; Luke 24.36b–48.

THE WITNESSING COMMUNITY

Worship Centre *The empty tomb.*

Music 'I know that my Redeemer liveth' from *Messiah* (Handel).

Call to Worship
Alleluia! Christ is risen!
Alleluia! He is risen indeed!
He unites us in heart and soul.
We share joy in his resurrection.
Sung Alleluia *Either* 'Alleluia, the Lord is risen' (see Appendix 1)
or the chorus of 'Good Christians all, rejoice and sing'

Adoration
God of history, we worship you.
You chose a nation to work for you.
You called prophets to tell people what you wanted.
You sent your chosen one, Jesus, to show people what you wanted.
We marvel that you made known your purposes for humanity.
We seek to respond to your will. We praise you for your love.
We rejoice that, in us, you awaken belief which enables us to
    respond,
strength which enables us to resist evil
and courage to witness to the power of your love
shown in the life, death and resurrection of Jesus Christ. **Amen.**

Confession
Forgive us, God our failure to respond to the witness
    of your people to the coming of the Christ.
For our lack of response: **In your mercy, forgive us.**
We have read what you say through the Bible and not understood:
For our lack of response: **In your mercy, forgive us.**
We have listened to the commandments and not obeyed:
For our lack of response: **In your mercy, forgive us.**
We have heard the challenge of the prophets and not paid attention:
For our lack of response: **In your mercy, forgive us.**

We have received the witness of the apostles and not passed it on:
For our lack of response: **In your mercy, forgive us.**
Enable us to be what is pure and to do what is right,
to be like Jesus, the Christ, who came to take away sins,
to be like Jesus, the Christ, in whom there was no sin.

Theme Prayer
God, the followers of Jesus were witnesses,
in their words and actions, to his risen life.
Help us so to recognize your power and his presence that our witness
may help people to become witnesses for themselves.

Act of Affirmation and Intercession
*Ask the congregation to suggest five groups of people (A–E) for
whom they would wish to show support in prayer. As the leader of the
prayer mentions each group in the phrase:* 'A (etc) ... stand very
firm!', *those who wish may stand (and remain standing for the rest of
the prayer) as all respond:* 'Stand firm: and see what the Lord can
do!' *(For a musical version of this response see p. 99).*

Thanksgiving
For the promises of freedom and community made to your chosen
   people of old:
For the healing power of your love: **Thank you, God.**
For the witness of prophet, priest and people to your word:
For the healing power of your love: **Thank you, God.**
For the promise of a new life in Jesus.
For the healing power of your love: **Thank you, God.**
For your new community, called through the love of Jesus:
For the healing power of your love: **Thank you, God.**
For the opportunity to belong to your community,
witnessing to your love in Jesus:
For the healing power of your love: **Thank you, God.**

Dismissal
The healing and the power of the Risen Christ be with you;
and the blessing of God ...

FOURTH SUNDAY OF EASTER

Acts 4.5–12; Psalm 23; I John 3.16–24; John 10.11–18.

THE CONFIDENT COMMUNITY

Worship Centre *Prepare a table on which signs of new life can be placed, e.g. spring flowers, twigs with green shoots, a baby's toy, something which represents a new community project.*

Call to Worship
Alleluia! Christ is risen!
Alleluia! He is risen indeed!
In him is our hope and our salvation.
We affirm our confidence in his resurrection.
Sung Alleluia *Either* 'Alleluia, the Lord is risen' (see Appendix 1)
or the chorus of 'Good Christians all, rejoice and sing'

Adoration
God of creation, you are in command.
We see and wonder at lengthening days,
with new life bursting from seed and egg, twig and bulb.
We hear the sounds of joy, the songs of birds, the buzzing of
insects, the shouts of children at play.
We smell the fresh day, we sense the crisp night.
We feel the warm returning sun, the cool spring showers.
We delight in new opportunities for being together and working
with one another in community.
This is a thrilling world. We are glad to be part of it.
The signs of new life are brought to the worship centre.
For who you are and what you have done for us, we adore you.

Confession
God, in this your world:
You give us control, yet we use it for selfish purposes.
Forgive us, God. **We are sorry, forgive us.**
You give us responsibility, yet we neglect to exercise it.
Forgive us, God. **We are sorry, forgive us.**
You show us compassion, yet we ignore need.
Forgive us, God. **We are sorry, forgive us.**
You gave yourself for us, yet we do not give ourselves for others.
Forgive us, God. **We are sorry, forgive us.**

God, renew our confidence in you, and grant us strength to be compassionate and unselfish, for Jesus sake. **Amen.**

Response and Reflection
Use the signs of new life which were placed on the worship centre. Initiate a conversation about the cycle of the seasons and of life in terms of hope and confidence in God, recognizing that at all stages of life there is the possibility of new life (not just in the spring). Reflect on the way seasonal imagery is used in hymns. What is it like to celebrate Easter in the southern hemisphere?

Prayer for the Offering
God, in the Risen Christ you have shown your power and given us hope. Set us free to use your gifts for the good of your world.

Thanksgiving
As the people of God we say:
  Thanks be to God.

We are the community of faith, confident
in the love of God,
in the life of God the Son,
in the power of God's Spirit:
As the people of God we say:
  Thanks be to God.

Trusting in the mercy of God,
changed by the love of Christ,
relying on the gift of the Spirit:
As the people of God we say:
  Thanks be to God.

God, love dwelling in us,
God, life given for us,
God, power working through us:
As your people we say:
  Thanks be to God.

Dismissal
The compassion and the strength of the Risen Christ be with you:
and the blessing of God ...

FIFTH SUNDAY OF EASTER

Acts 8.26–40; Psalm 22.25–31; I John 4.7–21; John 15.1–8.

THE MISSIONING COMMUNITY

Worship Centre *Arrange on table, placed centrally, twelve bunches of seedless grapes, sufficient for distribution later.*

Call to Worship
Alleluia! Christ is risen!
Alleluia! He is risen indeed!
In him is love and life for the world.
He is the Saviour of the world.
Sung Alleluia *Either* 'Alleluia, the Lord is risen' (see Appendix 1)
or the chorus of 'Good Christians all, rejoice and sing'

Adoration
(Child) This multi-coloured planet earth is God's;
         This multi-coloured human race is God's.
(Adult) We praise you, God.
         We worship you for what you have given all people.
(Child) Praise be for our mother earth;
         Praise be for our brothers and sisters on earth.
(Adult) We praise you, God.
         We worship you for what you have given all people.
(Child) Praise God for Jesus your Son, coming to earth;
         Praise God for Jesus, dying for us.
(Adult) We praise you, God.
         We worship you for what you have given all people.
(Child) Praise God for the Spirit, moving across the earth;
         Praise God for your Spirit, giving us life.
(Adult) We praise you, God.
         We worship you for what you have given all people.
(Child) We are your people, called to tell this Good News.
(Adult) We praise you, God.
         We worship you for what you have given all people.

Confession
(Child) God, we are excited that Jesus lives;
         We want to let others know about him.
(Adult) For our reluctance to tell others.
         God, in your love: **Forgive us, we pray.**

(Child)	We want to be known as his followers;
(Adult)	For our failure to be so
	God, in your love: **Forgive us, we pray.**
(Child)	We want to share our experience of him.
(Adult)	For our hesitation to do so
	God, in your love: **Forgive us, we pray.**
(Child)	You send us into the whole world.
(Adult)	For our unwillingness to go
	God, in your love: **Forgive us, we pray.**
(Child)	You have shown your love to us in Jesus.
(Adult)	Send us out in your Spirit to share your love.

Thanksgiving

God, we thank you that the friends of Jesus did not keep the good news he was alive to themselves and that they let his love flow through to give new life.

As an acting out of this prayer ask a group of people to distribute the bunches of grapes to the congregation until, in 'snowball' fashion, everyone has a sprig. During the distribution, a hymn or chorus could be sung. After the distribution the prayer concludes:

For the good news that Jesus lives:
   Thanks be to God, Alleluia!
For the life that we share in Jesus:
   Thanks be to God, Alleluia!
For the chance to make friends for Jesus:
   Thanks be to God, Alleluia!
For the power to change through Jesus:
   Thanks be to God, Alleluia!
For the new world brought in by Jesus:
   Thanks be to God, Alleluia!
With gratitude we respond.
Help us to go where you send us to tell others;
to make known your love by loving one another;
and to show our common life by word and deed. **Amen.**

Prayer at the Offering

Jesus, you are the true vine and we are the branches.
Help us to bear the fruit of your love in our lives.

Dismissal

The love and the life of the Risen Christ be with you:
and the blessing of God ...

SIXTH SUNDAY OF EASTER

Acts 10.44–48; Psalm 98; I John 5.1–6; John 1.9–17.

THE INCLUSIVE COMMUNITY

Worship Centre *Display a montage of flags, emblems, symbols which signify the vision of the breaking down of barriers between peoples, such as those of the United Nations, the Olympic Games, the European Community.*

Call to Worship
Alleluia! Christ is risen!
Alleluia! He is risen indeed!
In Christ is the truth that unites all peoples.
We rejoice that all are children of God.

Everyone shares a greeting. The call to worship then concludes:

Sung Alleluia *Either* 'Alleluia, the Lord is risen' (see Appendix 1) *or* the chorus of 'Good Christians all, rejoice and sing'

Adoration
Creator God, you have given us the privilege of life.
We praise you: **We adore you for this precious gift.**
We have the thrill of love, to love and to be loved.
We praise you: **We adore you for this precious gift.**
We have the ability to get to know each other.
We praise you: **We adore you for this precious gift.**
We have the possibility of being one community in one world.
We praise you: **We adore you for this precious gift.**
For the gift of Jesus, who calls us friends and calls us to be friends.
We praise you: **We adore you for this precious gift.**

Confession and Absolution
Gracious God, you love us all, whatever we are like.
We confess with shame how difficult we find it to love others as you love us.
When we find it hard to get along with those who are not like us:
God, in your mercy, forgive us.
When we speak to those we know and ignore those we don't:
God, in your mercy, forgive us.

When we relax in the presence of those who are like us and are ill at ease with those who aren't:
God, in your mercy, forgive us.
When we give generously to those in need far away and pass by those on our pavements:
God, in your mercy, forgive us.
When we accept those who look like us and turn away from those who seem different:
God, in your mercy, forgive us.
When we welcome those who adopt our ways of living and reject those who don't:
God, in your mercy, forgive us.
When we let differences of age, gender, race or religion, country or culture separate us:
God, in your mercy, forgive us.
Pause
This is love: not that we love God, but that God loves us.
We love because God first loved us.
In the name of Jesus Christ, your sins are forgiven.
Thanks be to God. Amen.
Sing 'Ubi caritas'

Theme Prayer
Lord, you have made yourself known to us
and have called us all your friends.
Send us out, as your chosen people
So that we may share your love through all the world.
We pray in your name. **Amen.**

Thanksgiving
God, we thank you for enriching our lives;
for all your gifts, and for our unity in Christ: **Thank you, God.**
For varieties of ability contributing to our well-being;
for all your gifts, and for our unity in Christ: **Thank you, God.**
For contrasts of views drawing us nearer the truth;
for all your gifts, and for our unity in Christ: **Thank you, God.**
For diversities of personality enlarging our vision;
for all your gifts, and for our unity in Christ: **Thank you, God.**
For reconciliation made possible through the Cross and Resurrection;
for all your gifts, and for our unity in Christ: **Thank you, God.**

Dismissal
The grace and the fellowship of the Risen Christ be with you:
and the blessing of God ...

SEVENTH SUNDAY OF EASTER

Acts 1.15–17, 21-26; Psalm 1; I John 5. 9–13; John 17. 6–19.

THE WAITING COMMUNITY

Worship Centre *A variety of objects which symbolise aspects of waiting: e.g.* birth, *a part knitted baby's garment, a baby chair;* death, *a bottle of pills, a will form:* new stage of life, *a pension book, a passport, a nurse's belt;* waiting for release, *a social security form, a rusty chain, an old leather belt.*

Call to Worship
Alleluia! Christ is risen!
Alleluia! He is risen indeed!
God has given us eternal life,
and this life is in his Son.
Sung Alleluia *Either* 'Alleluia, the Lord is risen' (see Appendix 1)
or the chorus of 'Good Christians all, rejoice and sing'

Prayer of Praise
God, we do not yet see the glory that you plan for all humankind:
But we do see Jesus,
and we thank you for the openness and patience,
the humility and wholeness,
in which Jesus lived and died for us,
and for that sympathy, that sharing with us
which makes our feelings and struggles heard,
and gives us boldness to follow in faith.
So let the earth break out in glory
and let the people shout for joy.
Cry, all creation, 'Holy', 'Holy',
'Holy is the Lord'! **Amen.**

Ministry of the Word
Ask people to talk in groups of two or three about their experiences of waiting. Read Acts 1.15–17, 21–26, introducing it by explaining that it describes how the disciples used the waiting time between the Ascension and the Day of Pentecost. In the light of the reading ask the groups to share their response as to how the disciples dealt with the waiting time and how that connects with their own experiences.

Theme Prayer
You never weary, Lord, of doing us good.
Let us never be weary of being in your service.
As you have pleasure in the prosperity of your servants,
so let us take pleasure in the service of our Lord,
and take pleasure in your love and praise, which never end.
Fill up all that is wanting and reform whatever is amiss.
Make us perfect in all that concerns your ways,
and in your forgiving love, dwell for ever in our hearts. **Amen.**
(from John Wesley)

Prayers for Those who Wait
God of all hope: **Help us all to know you in waiting.**
We pray for those who those spending time in waiting rooms,
waiting for treatment, waiting for news, waiting to help.
God of all hope: **Help us all to know you in waiting.**
We pray for those who wait to hear from loved ones,
longing for news, fearing the worst, hoping for the best.
God of all hope: **Help us all to know you in waiting.**
We pray for those who wait for a birth,
making room for new life, worrying if everything will be all right.
God of all hope: **Help us all to know you in waiting.**
We pray for those who wait for death,
fearful of the future, facing up to pain, celebrating life.
God of all hope: **Help us all to know you in waiting.**
We pray for those who wait for a new stage of life,
taking up new jobs, facing new challenges, preparing for retirement.
God of all hope: **Help us all to know you in waiting.**
We pray for those who wait for release,
existing in poverty, enduring prison, suffering abuse or neglect.
God of all hope: **Help us all to know you in waiting.**
We pray for those who have given up hope,
waiting for something to turn up, waiting in pain which seems
    endless.
God of all hope: **Help us all to know you in waiting.**
Loving God, we pray for this community as we wait for your Spirit
    to bring us life.
God of all hope: **Help us all to know you in waiting.**

Dismissal
The hope of the Risen Christ be with you:
and the blessing ...

PENTECOST

Acts 2.1–21 *or* Ezekiel 37.1–14; Psalm 104.23–34, 35*b*;
Romans 8.22–27 *or* Acts 2.1–21; John 15.26–27; 16.4b–15.

THE SPIRIT AS THE BREATH OF GOD

Worship Centre *Use symbols of wind/breath: flute or recorder, garden chimes, children's windmill, candle burning, fan (switched on and blowing) tall grasses, etc.*

Call to Worship *(Psalm 104.30)*
Send forth your Spirit, O Lord, and renew the face of the earth.

Opening Responses
Holy Spirit, come among us:
  Amen ! We meet in Jesus' name.
Like the light of day, shine on us:
  Come, bring us into your glory.
Free as a bird, settle among us:
  Amen ! Come ! Cover us with your mercy.
Like a mighty wind, inspire us:
  Come, create your new life in us.
Dancing like a flame, kindle our hearts:
  Order our ways and set us free.
Holy Spirit, come to be in us:
  Amen! Come!

Prayer of Approach and Invocation
Breathe here and now: remember us,
  and send on us your surging light.
Welcome, Mother of the poor,
  welcome, bearer of our comfort,
  welcome, you who seek our good.
Gentlest of all, drying our tears,
  our friend, our shadow,
  the place for rest in our drudge and toil,
  the breathing space in our handicaps.
You are God: without you, we are out of joint.
You are God: soothe our wounds.
  Give water to our withered roots: make us new.
  In the Spirit, and in Jesus' name, we make our prayer. **Amen.**

64

Liturgical Dance
Ask a group of different ages to dance using pieces of light material, ribbon or chiffon scarves. For music use the melody of a song about the Holy Spirit played on a wind instrument.

Litany for Pentecost *(to be read after the Gospel)*
Come Holy Spirit: **Come Holy Spirit, speak to us.**
Speak to us in the language of our need:
when we feel downhearted and unloved,
Come Holy Spirit: **Come Holy Spirit, speak to us.**
Speak to us in the language of our hopes:
when we dream dreams and have visions,
Come Holy Spirit: **Come Holy Spirit, speak to us.**
Speak to us in the language of our fear:
when we are scared of the future and worried about one another,
Come Holy Spirit: **Come Holy Spirit, speak to us.**
Speak to us in the language of our hearts:
when we want to feel your presence around and within us,
Come Holy Spirit: **Come Holy Spirit, speak to us.**

Prayer of Thanksgiving
Holy One, we hear your music in the roar of the sea,
in the song of a people,
in the quiet breeze rustling through the trees.
We thank you God: **That you so love our world.**

Holy One, we sense your power in the flickering of fire,
in the yearning of our spirits,
in the dispelling of shadows.
We thank you God: **That you so love our world.**

Holy One, we feel your caress in the gift of our humanity,
in our desire to be whole,
in the blessing of peace.
We thank you God: **That you so love our world.**

Prayer of Offering
Go on your way, and live in the presence of God's Holy Spirit,
that what needs to change may be changed through God's grace,
that what needs strengthening may be strengthened in God's love,
that you may be instruments through which God's music is heard;
to the praise of Jesus Christ our Lord. **Amen.**

TRINITY SUNDAY

Isaiah. 6.1–8; Psalm 29; Romans 8.12–17; John 3.1–17.

THE CIRCLE OF GOD'S LOVE

Worship Centre Either: *a representation of the Icon of the Trinity (The Hospitality of Abraham) by Rublev with a circle in front* or: *an enlarged picture of a Celtic knot (perhaps on an overhead projector) with, in front of it, the same circular picture; in either case place three unlit candles within the circle.*

Call to Worship (*Isaiah 6.3*)
Holy, holy, holy, God of love and giver of life:
all that is in earth and heaven gives you glory.

Invocation (*for three readers standing by the candles*)
A, B, C: Let us praise God
The first candle is lit
A   We light a flame in the name of God
    who sets the sun and stars in the circle of the heavens.
The second candle is lit
B   We light a flame in the name of God
    whose outstretched arms embrace us all.
The third candle is lit
C   We light a flame in the name of God
    who draws us into a circle of love.

Prayer of Approach (*Romans 8.12–17*)
Encircling God, surrounding us – Creator, Son, Spirit:
You are our God and you give us life.
Encircling God, surrounding us in love,
Calling us to become your children, not as slaves.
We share in your suffering and the hope of your glory,
yet to be born.
Encircling God, hold us in your love.

Dance
Invite children to dance in a circle while everyone sings 'God has put a circle round us'.

Ministry of the Word
Invite people to talk about different ways in which the Trinity has been portrayed. Either use the symbolism of the Celtic knot, or look

at the representation of the icon, noting that the angels who have come to bring the news of a child to Sarah are placed in the shape of a circle, with the chalice at the centre. In the latter case use the following:

Three in one, in closest harmony,
Circled by love, in tender symmetry
Offering up the Lamb who is to be
Life for the world.

Angels are they, yet hold in meaning more
Than angels visiting at Sarah's door :
God's life itself, ready for us to pour
Grace on this world.

Help us then this circle now to join,
Our lives in newborn harmony entwine,
In action mirroring the life divine
Revealed in our world.

Thanksgiving
Blessed are you, God: Spirit of Creation!
You moved across the void,
shaping form out of chaos,
pulsating light in darkness,
energizing life out of dust.

Blessed are you, God: Spirit of Redemption!
You came to your own world,
becoming flesh for those in the control of evil,
becoming light for those in the ways of darkness,
becoming life to those in the shadow of death.

Blessed are you, God: Spirit of Renewal!
You flow into this age,
breathing life into those who believe,
streaming power into those who receive,
kindling love in those who respond.

Dismissal
God sends us out into the world
to accept the cost, and to discover the joy of discipleship.
Therefore, go – carrying with you
the peace of Christ, the love of God
and the encouragement of the Holy Spirit,
in trial and rejoicing: and the blessing of God ...

SUNDAY BETWEEN 29 MAY AND 4 JUNE
Ninth Sunday in Ordinary Time

I Samuel 3.1–20; Psalm 139.1–6, 13–18;
or Deuteronomy 5.12–15; Psalm 81.1–10.
II Corinthians 4.5–12; Mark 2.23–3.6.

STILLNESS IN GOD

Worship Centre *A cloth, candle and single flower on a table.*

Opening Song 'Speak, Lord in the stillness'.

Prayer of Approach *Focus on the worship centre for the prayer.*

Be still and know the God we worship ...
Be still and know ...
Be still ...
Silence
Loving God, we have gathered to meet you.
We have come to listen to you
to seek you, to worship you.
You are the beginning of all things,
the life of all things, you knew us before we were born.
In you we become, in you we live.
Loving God, you are here and everywhere,
around us and within us, you know our inmost thoughts.
In you we hope, in you we live.
You are the source of serenity,
giving peace which is beyond our understanding.
In you we are still, in you we live.
Loving God, we live in you, we worship you.
Loving God, you live in us, we worship you.
Silence

Holy God, eternal,
out of whose darkness galaxies spin into brilliance
and in whose openness the universe is hidden:
centre our restlessness in the silent music of eternity
that we may hear you calling us out,
to be and to become, made perfect in your love. **Amen.**

Ministry of the Word

Read I Samuel 3.1–20 in dramatized form using a small child for Samuel and an older man for Eli.

Confession/Meditation *(following I Samuel 3.1–20)*

Lord, we think we are seeking you but you are seeking us.

We think that prayer is about talking to you but you want to talk with us.

Lord we are here:

Speak Lord, we are listening.

Silence

Lord, there is no time to listen, no time for silence, no time to listen for your voice.

Life is frantic, noisy, rushing; we are too busy for you.

Lord we are here:

Speak Lord, we are listening.

Silence

Lord, when we hear your purpose clearly but resist,

Let your gentleness be strong enough to break through.

We want to love and serve you.

Lord we are here:

Speak Lord, we are listening.

Silence

As you look into our hearts and minds we acknowledge our need for healing and forgiveness.

We acknowledge our unwillingness to be still in you.

We acknowledge our unreadiness to listen to you.

Lord we are here:

Speak Lord, we are listening.

Dismissal

God says 'Before I formed you in the womb I knew you.'

In the silence of the womb we were known by God.

In our stillness now may we know God.

Let us listen to God:

Let us hear God:

Now and always. **Amen.**

SUNDAY BETWEEN 5 AND
11 JUNE   Tenth Sunday in Ordinary Time

I Samuel 8.4–11,16–20; Psalm 138;
or Genesis 3.8–15; Psalm 130;
II Corinthians 4.13–5:1; Mark 3.20–35.

PUTTING GOD FIRST

Sung Call to Worship
'Come all you people, come and praise your maker'

Responsive Greetings *(based on Psalm 138)*
Praise the Lord with all your heart!
   We come to sing praises to God.
Come and sing your praises to God!
   For the glory of God is great.
The glory of God is great!
   God's love lasts for ever.
The love of God is everlasting!
   We praise God with all our heart.

Prayer of Approach *(The Collect for Purity)*
   Almighty God,
   to whom all hearts are open,
   all desires known,
   and from whom no secrets are hidden:
   cleanse the thoughts of our hearts
   by the inspiration of your Holy Spirit,
   that we may perfectly love you,
   and worthily magnify your holy Name;
   through Christ our Lord. Amen.

Adoration and Confession
Merciful God
   Your love is greater than anything we can understand.
   Your power is greater than we can imagine.
   Your forgiveness is beyond our comprehension.

The world is full of wonder: too often we fail to see it.
   We have been given the capacity to love,
      too often we love only ourselves.
   We believe and speak of you,
      too often we forget you in our lives.

Forgive us for the unseeing times
Forgive us for the un-loving times
Forgive us for the forgetful times.
Silence
Enfold us in your love
Make us true to you
Perceiving, loving and remembering through Jesus
all that you have made and all that you have done.
We thank you. **Amen.**

Song *(best used after the lessons. It is sung to the tune 'Green grow the rushes O!' and will need practice by the song leader to make sure how the words fit.)*
Who knows what one is? Who can tell the mystery?
I know who one is:
God is One and God alone is worthy of all worship!
Who knows what two is? Who can tell the mystery?
I know what two is:
Two, two the testaments, telling of God's faithfulness:
God is One and God alone is worthy of all worship!
Who knows what three is? Who can tell the mystery?
I know what three is:
Three-in-One, the Trinity!
Two, two the testaments, telling of God's faithfulness:
God is One and God alone is worthy of all worship!

And so on, until:

Who knows infinity? Who can tell the mystery?
I know infinity:
God's great love is without end, while
Seven are the days of every week,
Six are half the apostles,
Five are the books of Moses,
Four are the Gospel stories,
Three-in-One, the Trinity!
Two, two the testaments, telling of God's faithfulness:
God is One and God alone is worthy of all worship!

Donald Pickard

Prayer before Dismissal
God of understanding,
help us to grasp the truth about Jesus.
Help us to follow him in sincerity and truth,
that we may be his mother, sister, brother. **Amen.**

SUNDAY BETWEEN 12 AND 18

JUNE   Eleventh Sunday in Ordinary Time

I Samuel 15.34–16.13; Psalm 20;
or Ezekiel 17.22–24; Psalm 92.1–4, 12–15.
II Corinthians 6–10, 14–17; Mark 4:26–34.

PREPARED BY GOD

Worship Centre *Two parcels placed on a table – one beautifully wrapped but full of old newspaper, one wrapped simply in plain brown paper but containing something nice e.g. sweets or fruit.*

Call to Worship (*from Psalm 92*)
It is good to give thanks to you, Lord,
to sing praises to your name, O Most High,
to declare your steadfast love in the morning.
At the works of your hands we sing for joy.

Prayer of Praise
For tiny seeds which grow into mighty trees,
Creator God, we praise you: we trust you!
For young babies who become boys and girls, women and men,
Creator God, we praise you: we trust you!
For bright ideas which lead to wider vision,
Creator God, we praise you: we trust you!
For fresh opportunities which lead in unknown directions,
Creator God, we praise you: we trust you!
For small beginnings which become great challenges,
Creator God, we praise you: we trust you!

Activity (*to precede the I Samuel reading*)
Ask people to choose which parcel they would like to receive. Get a group to come forward to choose one to open. What did they base their choice on? Then open the second one. Had they made to right choice? If not, why not? Things are not always as they seem. God looks inside. David was not the obvious choice for a king. Why did God choose him?

72

Prayer of Confession and Thanks
Creating God,
you see all there is to see,
you know all there is to know,
you sustain us in all we do,
Forgive us for thinking that we can sustain ourselves.

Forgiving God,
you know us inside out.
Help us when we look at others
not to look with our own eyes but as you would.
May we judge not by earthly standards, but by yours.

Renewing God,
you know us from the inside
better than we know ourselves.
You see us and know us. **Thank you, Lord.**

Renewing God,
you never leave us alone,
you hold us and support us.
You see us and know us. **Thank you, Lord.**

Renewing God,
you are there when we are growing secretly,
you are there as we grow to maturity.
You see us and know us. **Thank you, Lord.**

Meditation (*to follow the Gospel*)
The seed is scattered on the ground.
Deep in the earth, watered by rain, warmed by sun
it grows, secretly, unseen except by God.

No one sees it happen,
no one knows when it will happen,
but secretly, unseen, a shoot appears.

As the seed grows the plant becomes large and strong,
a tree, a place of strength and comfort,
a tree in which the birds can rest.

No one knows how it happens but God's time comes.
The seed of God's kingdom is sown secretly amongst us.
God's time will come.

Sing 'Just a Tiny Seed'

SUNDAY BETWEEN 19 AND 25 JUNE

Twelfth Sunday in Ordinary Time

I Samuel 17.32–49; Psalm 9.9–20;
or Job 38.1–11; Psalm 107.1–3, 23–32.
II Corinthians 6.1–13; Mark 4.35–41.

STRENGTH AND PEACE IN GOD

Worship Centre *A table covered with a large blue (or blue/grey, blue/green) cloth to represent the sea. At the beginning the cloth is smooth. Before the opening reading the cloth is rucked up in folds – it is smoothed out again after the reading (representing rough and calm water). The same sequence is followed for the reading of the Gospel.*

Music for worship *Fourth movement, 'The Storm' from Beethoven's Symphony no.6 in F major (The Pastoral).*

Opening Reading Psalm 107.23–32
Note the suggestion about the worship centre above.

Either
Story Meditation
The sea was calm when we set out.
It had been a busy day; it always was with Jesus around.
People followed us everywhere, he welcomed them, loved them.

It had been a busy day and Jesus was tired.
We'd heard him tell many stories, we'd seen a lot of people;
they loved him.

Jesus was tired and he lay down in the boat,
and rested his head on a cushion.
The sea was calm and he was soon asleep.

Suddenly a storm blew up. And what a storm!
The waves were lashing the boat, and throwing us up and down!
The boat was swamped and the wind blew so hard we couldn't keep
   control.
We shouted out, we were afraid, we thought we would drown.

And through it all, Jesus slept.
He slept on a cushion, calm and peaceful.
As the storm raged around us he didn't even notice.
He hadn't even noticed that we could drown!
In desperation we shook him awake.

Quietly, calmly, he spoke to the storm.
– Be still!
The sea was calm, and the wind had ceased.
Where is your faith? he asked us.
We were more unnerved by this calm than by the storm.
Who is this man?

Or
Story Song (*with actions – encourage everyone to join in*)
'One day when we were fishing'

Confession
God of calm and power, why do we not trust you?
Your power stills the storms, overcomes giants.
Why do we fail to recognize you?
Forgive us when we do not recognize you.

We know that you are there.
We recall your promise to be with us everywhere.
Why are we surprised that you are?
Forgive us when we are surprised by your power.

We tell of your wonders, we sing your praises.
Sometimes we are so self-confident that we manage alone.
At other times we are so lacking in confidence that we do not even
    begin.
Forgive us when we fail to trust your strength.

'The Lord is a refuge for the oppressed,
a stronghold in times of trouble.
The Lord will never fail those who seek.'

Peace! Be still in the strength and power of the forgiveness of God.
Amen: Thanks be to God!

Dismissal
Go in peace, in the knowledge of God's power.
Go in confidence, in the knowledge of God's strength.
Go in joy, in the knowledge of God's love.

SUNDAY BETWEEN 26 JUNE AND 2 JULY
Thirteenth Sunday in Ordinary Time

II Samuel 1.1,17–27; Psalm 130 *or* Lamentations 3.23–33;
or Wisdom 1.13–15, 2.23–24; Psalm 30.
II Corinthians 8.7–15; Mark 5.21–43.

RHYTHMS OF LIFE (1): LIFE AND DEATH

Worship Centre *A display of items commonly lost such as keys, a purse/wallet, a ring, a 'well-loved' cuddly toy, along with a photograph of somebody now dead such as a grandparent of the worship leader, or a famous public figure.*

Call to Worship

Jesus Christ is risen.	**God's love is new each morning.**
He shares our laughter.	**God's love is new each morning.**
He cries when we cry.	**God's love is new each morning.**
He calls us to worship.	**God's love is new each morning.**

Prayer of Praise

God of life, yours is the power that forged the universe.
Yours is the skill that gave birth to creatures large and small, making our earth a garden for your joy, and for us a hint of heaven.
We love you so much: **Lead us into life.**
God of life, yours is the love that keeps hope alive for the world.
It feels amazing to us – and painful – to be human, capable of love; capable of loving you and one another with a fierceness which still surprises us.
We love you so much: **Lead us into life.**
God of life, yours is the energy that makes all things complete.
You make old things new, broken relationships whole, weak people strong; deep wounds are healed and failed lives ready to start again.
We love you so much: **Lead us into life.**

Ministry of the Word

Talk about the items in the worship centre, then about who has lost any of them or other precious things, and how it felt, especially when they were never found. In twos or threes share experiences of grief over the death of family members or friends. From this reflect in the biblical stories: the feelings of David at the loss of Jonathan or of Jairus and his daughter's illness.

An Act of Remembrance

Jesus, hearing the stories of you with people grieving, brings to mind for us memories of those we have loved and who have died. And it hurts.

Often we have felt we must hide our feelings and grieve alone.
People tell us to be strong, and that the strong do not cry.
Yet you have shown us that to live life fully can be to get hurt and feel pain.
You wept with the crowds at Lazarus' grave,
and you joined the mourners in the home of Jairus.

In the presence of each other we remember those who have died, who were dear to us.
We thank you for all that delighted us about them, and made them special to us.
We thank you for the life we shared with them and for all they gave to us.
So we thank you for our memories,
and even for the mixture of joy and sadness they give,
teaching us that love is stronger than death.

Play some suitable recorded music (e.g. The 'Pié Jesu' from a Requiem: Fauré or Lloyd Webber) and invite people during this time to light candles in thankfulness for particular friends remembered.

Thank you, Jesus our friend, for sharing friendship with us through other people.
Thank you for the example of their living and for the inspiration they have given us.

God our Father we bless you, and we offer to you all our feelings:
our gladness and sadness, our pride and regret,
our hope and our longing, and our trust in you, even when our faith falls short.
We rejoice in your perfect love for the living and the dead,
And we bless you because we can know your love through others.
May we hear your strong voice say to us: 'Go in Peace'. **Amen.**

Dismissal

Go in peace: for the God of Peace goes with you. **Amen.**

SUNDAY BETWEEN 3 AND 9 JULY

Fourteenth Sunday in Ordinary Time

II Samuel 5.1–5, 9–10; Psalm 48;
or Ezekiel 2.1–5; Psalm 123.
II Corinthians 12.2–10; Mark 6.1–13.

RHYTHMS OF LIFE (2): COMING HOME

Worship Centre *Display posters around the church with well-known sayings about home (e.g. 'Home Sweet Home', 'There's no place like home', 'Home is where the heart is').*

Music for Worship *Listen to a secular/popular song/poem which is about leaving, being away from home or coming home.*

Reflection
Play 'Desert Island Homes'. Each person should reflect on what six items they would take to a desert island to help it feel like home. (If there is time ask, 'Which one of the six would be most significant in terms of home?') Thoughts could be shared in groups or one or more persons could be interviewed.

Prayer of Thanksgiving
God, it is good to come home.
We thank you for the excitement of journeys, for the joy of discovery, the thrill of new experiences, the delight of new sights and sounds, and the pleasure of new places.
Thank you for stretching the bounds of our imagination and enlarging our vision.
For journeys and for coming home: **Thank you, God.**

Thank you, God, for familiar things.
For the well-worn sofa, the coffee mug which all the family knows is ours, the squeaky floorboard, the photographs on the shelf, rain on the window, the family pet, the comfort of our own bed at day's end.
For familiar things which speak to us of home: **Thank you, God.**

Thank you, God, for family and friends.
For those who live with us, those who come to stay, those who turn up as a surprise on our doorsteps, those whom we go to visit and whose homes feel like our home, and those we long for and from whom we are separated.
For people with whom we feel at home: **Thank you, God.**

78

Thank you, God, for all whom we love, and for your own friendship through Jesus.

For comfort in our hurting, for encouragement in our work, for togetherness in our celebrations, for forgiveness in our failures.

For the knowledge that in new and old, in the strange and the familiar and, after all our journeying, you are ready to welcome us and bring us home. **Amen.**

Prayer for Others and Ourselves
Use a sung response: 'Domine Deus' or a Taizé 'Kyrie'

God, who waits for the wanderers to come home, we pray for all those who today are returning home. For those celebrating joyful homecomings, those discharged from hospital or released from prison, those returning from working away, those planning to move into new homes, those restored into healed relationships. **Response.**

God, who was born among us far from home, we pray for all the homeless and for refugees. We pray for young people abused at home or turned out of home, and for all who have returned home and found backs turned on them. **Response.**

God, who is everywhere at home, we pray for those for whom home is a mixed blessing. We pray for all who find that home sometimes constricts them rather than setting them free, those whose lives revolve around caring for dependent relatives, elderly parents or young children. We pray for Christians who struggle to live in faith with those who do not share their faith. **Response.**

God, your grace is sufficient for us; we dedicate our homes to you. May they be open homes where love is freely shared. May we learn within them the arts of hospitality. Wherever you call us may we journey in faith, so that others might find their true home with you. **Response.**

Dismissal
May the life-giving Spirit and the friendship of Jesus
make all of our meeting and all of our sharing
a sign of God's way:
and wherever we travel may God's blessing be with us:
in laughter and crying,
in coming and going,
on the road and at home. **Amen.**

SUNDAY BETWEEN 10 AND 16

JULY   Fifteenth Sunday in Ordinary Time

II Samuel 6.1–5,12b–19; Psalm 24;
or Amos 7.7–1; Psalm 85.8–13.
Ephesians 1.3–14; Mark 6.14–29.

RHYTHMS OF LIFE (3): HAPPY AND UNHAPPY ENDINGS

Worship Centre *A tree in a pot (or a large painted tree) and a dustbin.*

Opening Affirmation *(based on Psalm 24)*
Use this dialogue outside the church, at the beginning of the service.
A   This is God's planet. God made every part of it.
B   We are God's people; every one of us on earth.
A   How shall come into God's house to worship?
B   We come offering actions and thoughts which are good and pure,
A   wanting God to be first in our lives.
B   always at our side working on our behalf.
A & B   Let us worship together, offering ourselves -
        Fling the doors open in joyful welcome!

Activities
Either *(following the Old Testament and the Epistle)* Dreams and Disasters. *Each writes a cherished dream on a gift tag to hang on the tree (if you have a painted tree use 'post-it' notes). Each person also writes on a different piece of paper words or phrases relating to a hard experience they have had. After a silence, people bring their dreams to the tree, tearing up the other paper and putting the pieces into the dustbin.*

Or *(following the reading of the Gospel)* Happy and Sad Endings. *The congregation talk to each other about a favourite film or book, and whether 'happy ever after' or sad endings make the best stories. Finally consider whether John the Baptist was a tragic figure or not, and use the Meditation.*

Meditation
We all like a happy ending.
It's good to cry because it all turned out even better than we hoped, even though it's just a story!

When the episode of our favourite soap ends with disaster
we watch tomorrow knowing a plot will be woven from it –
otherwise we would stop watching!

Real life isn't so tidy.
From some disasters there is no way back to normality.
The lives of some limp from disappointment to disappointment.
Every fear seems realized; never a dream comes true.

It can be hard to believe in a God of happy endings
– when God's faithful prophet suffers execution to satisfy a king's
rash promise.
It can be hard to believe in a God who promises that 'righteousness
and peace will kiss each other',
– when the queen resents the truth
and the party becomes a place of horror,
and the joyful dance turns quickly to tragedy.
What kind of plan could be worth such sacrifice?
Does every execution lead to resurrection?
But we believe in God,
whose foolishness is wiser than our wisdom
and whose purposes are not limited by our wish for happy endings.
In hope and in doubt God is with us.
Thanks be to God.

Act of Trust and Commitment
Dancing can be so puzzling.
The individual steps of life may make little sense taken alone.
But you, Lord, are the choreographer: fill the universe with dance.
Lord of the dance: **Teach us to dance with you.**

Dancing can be so ambiguous.
We may be afraid to take part, lest we get the wrong message, or,
    like Herod, are led astray.
But you, Lord, are the interpreter: reveal each movement in life's
    dance to us.
Lord of the dance: **Teach us to dance with you.**

Dancing can be so powerful.
It makes deep impressions and stirs deep emotions.
But you, Lord, are the principal dancer: lead all our feet so that we
    might all be in step with you.
Lord of the dance: **Teach us to dance with you.**

SUNDAY BETWEEN 17 AND 23

JULY   Sixteenth Sunday in Ordinary Time

II Samuel 7.1–14a; Psalm 89.20–37;
or Jeremiah 23.1–6; Psalm 23.
Ephesians 2.11–22; Matthew 13.24–30, 36–43.

RHYTHMS OF LIFE (4): WORK AND REST

Worship Centre *Two displays, one of work 'tools' or other symbols of the 'working' lives of the congregation, the other containing symbols of holidays, time off and hobbies.*

Prayer of Confession
Lord Jesus, you lived a life in harmony: rest and work, time for others and time for yourself, activity and prayer, were in perfect balance. We often get it wrong.
When we work so hard that there is no time for those we love:
Lord, forgive us. **Lord, forgive.**
When we view our work purely in terms of what we have achieved:
Lord, forgive us. **Lord, forgive.**
When all our busy-ness fails to make sense:
Lord, forgive us. **Lord, forgive.**
When we linger too long by still waters knowing you've called us into the dark valley:
Lord, forgive us. **Lord, forgive.**
When we forget in our work or play that you are with us:
Lord, forgive us. **Lord, forgive.**
Thank you Lord for your patience and encouragement with us in all we do: Thank you for leading us in your way. **Amen.**

Meditation *(following the Epistle)*
Play quiet background music. People are invited to look at fixtures and people around the church as the meditation proceeds.
Let us take time to feel good about what God has done for us.
Pause (at least half a minute)
We were strangers to the rich history and amazing promises of God towards his people. Now we are where God wants us to be, right at the heart of things.
Pause
Jesus, by the breaking of his body and the shedding of his blood, brings us peace: peace without limit, peace for all, peace with God.
Pause

In Christ we are all equal. There is no room for division between those who are loved by God our Father.

Pause

Whoever we are and whatever we were, God joins us to each other and builds us all up. In Christ we belong and belong together, a home for the Spirit of God.

Prayers of Thanksgiving

The congregation works in groups to prepare prayers of thanks.

Activity group 1 *Holidays. Children say what they enjoy about long school holidays. All ages share favourite destinations, or identify with a symbol in the worship centre. The group makes suggestions for thank you prayers.*

Activity group 2 *Work. Children describe aspects of school they enjoy and young people share career dreams. Everyone identifies enjoyable aspects of their daily life in a way that affirms all kinds of work (the items in the worship centre may help with this). The group makes suggestions for thank you prayers.*

Litany of Blessing

Invite each person to identify with one or more of the groups mentioned and therefore not to join in that response. (Omit any bidding inappropriate to the congregation.) Encourage people to look at those they are blessing.

Pre-school children and babies in the womb, in all your exploring:

We bless you and offer to God the work of your hands and hearts.

Children at school, in your widening horizons and growing minds:

We bless you and offer to God the work of your hands and hearts.

Young people, wondering what the world of work holds, in your searching and preparing:

We bless you and offer to God the work of your hands and hearts.

Carers, home-makers, volunteers and befrienders, whose work is unpaid and not always appreciated, in your moments of richness and of frustration:

We bless you and offer to God the work of your hands and hearts.

You, employed or self-employed, seeking to change your work, or looking for employment, in your struggles and in your fulfilment:

We bless you and offer to God the work of your hands and hearts.

You whom the world calls retired, but who use all your energies and interests creatively, in your praying and witnessing:

We bless you and offer to God the work of your hands and hearts.

SUNDAY BETWEEN 24 AND 30
JULY — Seventeenth Sunday in Ordinary Time

II Samuel 11.1–15; Psalm 14;
or II Kings 4.42–44; Psalm 145.10–18.
Ephesians 3.14–2; John 6.1–21.

POWER THROUGH THE SPIRIT

Worship Centre *Display a net with loaves (bread rolls) and fishes
(either real or made from silver card).*

Approach
Come, let us worship.
God, you made us.
**We come with lips of praise,
with grateful hearts and ready minds, to hear your word.**

Adoration
God of hot days and warm nights:
> **We rejoice in your activity and receive your gifts.**
God of quiet hours and exciting days:
> **We rejoice in your activity and receive your gifts.**
God of rewarding work and relaxing leisure:
> **We rejoice in your activity and receive your gifts.**
God of holy days and holidays:
> **We rejoice in your activity and receive your gifts.**

Confession
We acknowledge, God, that you are generous:
> **Forgive our lack of generosity.**
You provide for our needs – yet we neglect others' needs:
> **Forgive our lack of generosity.**
You present us with gifts – yet we fail to use them wisely:
> **Forgive our lack of generosity.**
You treat us as friends – yet we keep that friendship to ourselves:
> **Forgive our lack of generosity.**
You grant us more than enough – yet we waste so much:
> **Forgive our lack of generosity.**

Jesus said: 'I have come that you may have life in all its fulness.'
May we receive graciously and share generously. **Amen.**

84

Ministry of the Word
*Act out the story of the feeding of the multitude by miming to the
reading or by a dramatized reading.*

Response
Either *Share bread as a sign of fellowship.*
Read John 6.11a.
*Hand the rolls from the worship centre to members of the congrega-
tion. Each person breaks off a piece and hands on to others, who
repeat the action until everyone has a piece. Following the eating of
the bread sing the first verse of the song: 'Jesus the Lord said, "I am
the bread"'.*
Or *An act of intercession.*
*Distribute in baskets pieces of paper in the shape of loaves or fishes.
Ask people to use them in the prayers of intercession by tracing with
their finger an appropriate name under each heading:* e.g. 'We pray
for ... (an individual) ... (a group) ... (a current concern or situation)
etc.' *End the prayers by collecting the loaves and fishes in the baskets.*

Theme Prayer
O God, whose Son, in the power of the Spirit, worked amongst
people, meeting need with compassionate love, grant that we, by the
same Spirit, may grasp the breadth, length, height and depth of your
love, and share in your work, in Jesus' name. **Amen.**

Thanksgiving
Gracious God, you provide for our needs and you use what we have
to meet the needs of others.
For crops of the soil and the produce of the sea:
We are grateful. **We thank you, God.**
For your gifts of compassion and energy which empower us to share
in feeding the hungry and refreshing the tired:
We are grateful. **We thank you, God.**
For your Spirit in creation, active to sustain us as we live and grow in
body, mind and spirit:
We are grateful. **We thank you, God.**
For the gift of peace as we put our trust in your presence and
unlimited resources:
We are grateful. **We thank you, God. Amen.**

Dismissal
Go in peace in the power of the Spirit to live and work for the glory
of God. **Amen.**

SUNDAY BETWEEN 31 JULY AND
6 AUGUST Eighteenth Sunday in Ordinary Time

II Samuel 1.26–12.13a; Psalm 51.1–12;
or Exodus 16.2–4, 9-15; Psalm 78.23–29.
Ephesians 4.1–16; John 6.24–35.

UNITY IN THE SPIRIT

Worship Centre *On a table, place a cloth and in the centre a loaf of bread (the table should be large enough for other bread rolls to be added during the act of worship).*

Approach
Come, let us worship.
God, you made us.
We come together to join in praise,
with grateful hearts and ready minds, to hear your word.

Adoration
We adore you, the one and only God,
the God of power and glory and holiness:
> although beyond us, you draw near to us,
> although separate from us, you are with us.
Accept, we pray, our wonder at you, our love for you.
We bring you our worship, as we respond to your love.

We marvel at the way you care for us:
you feed us when we are hungry,
you give us strength when we are weary,
you encourage us when we are sad.
We rejoice that you are always with us:
you lead us, both in easy and in difficult times,
you come to us even when we complain and grumble.
We celebrate your gifts to each one of us.
We adore you for your greatest gift, the gift of life. offered to us in
Jesus and known to us through your Spirit within us. **Amen.**

Confession
Let us confess our sins to God.
Silence
When we neglect you when things go well and blame you if things
   go wrong:
> Lord have mercy. **Christ have mercy.**

When we fail to be humble, gentle and patient:
Lord have mercy. **Christ have mercy.**
When we do not use your special gifts in the way you want:
Lord have mercy. **Christ have mercy.**
When we allow ourselves to be led astray from your ways:
Lord have mercy. **Christ have mercy.**
When we fail to stand up for the truth:
Lord have mercy. **Christ have mercy.**
When we do not try hard enough to be the People of God:
Lord have mercy. **Christ have mercy.**
Silence
God who calls you is faithful: be faithful to your calling.
In the name of Jesus Christ. **Amen.**

Activity
After the reading of the Gospel people bring up bread rolls and put them on the table. After each roll is placed one of the sentences from the Gospel is read and the congregation respond:
Christ is the bread of life.
Jesus said: 'I am the bread of life.'
Jesus said: 'It is my Father who gives you the true bread from
    heaven.'
Jesus said: 'The bread of God gives life to the world.'
Jesus said: 'Whoever comes to me will never be hungry, and
    whoever believes in me will never be thirsty.'
Jesus said: 'This is the work of God, that you believe in him whom
    God has sent.'

Thanksgiving
Thank you God for all your gifts:
for food from earth and food from heaven:
Thanks be to God.
For Jesus Christ, the bread of life:
Thanks be to God.
For the Holy Spirit, who binds us together in peace:
Thanks be to God.
For giving meaning to life now and beyond death:
Thanks be to God.
For equipping us to build the church as one in Christ:
Thanks be to God.
For challenging us to share the good news of your love:
Thanks be to God.
Thank you, God. You are over all and through all and in all.
Thank you God, for all your gifts, in Jesus Christ our Lord. **Amen.**

SUNDAY BETWEEN 7 AND 13
AUGUST Nineteenth Sunday in Ordinary Time

II Samuel 18.5–9,15, 31-3; Psalm 130;
or I Kings 19.4–8; Psalm 34.1–8.
Ephesians 4.25–5.2; John 6.35, 41–51.

SEAL OF THE SPIRIT

Worship Centre *A table prepared to display objects brought up during the worship. Behind the table a display board with bags from local shops stapled on to it.*

Approach
Come, let us worship.
God, you made us.
We come, marked by your Spirit,
with grateful hearts and ready minds, to hear your word.

Adoration
Everyday God, we come to worship you.
We come from the busyness of work, the enjoyment of leisure, the challenge of school, the responsibilities of home.
We come to meet with you and to be with each other, to acknowledge you as the Creator who bothers about each one of us.
We are amazed that you have such a concern and a care for this world, which is so small in the vastness of the universe. For us you took the incredible step to be with us in your Son. He gave his life for us and lives in us today through the Spirit.
We bring you astonished adoration, wonder and praise.
We are silent before you as we reflect upon what you have done.
To you, Father, Son and Spirit, be glory for ever! **Amen.**

Confession (*as an alternative response sing a 'Kyrie Eleison'*)
Challenging God, you call us into the way of Jesus to be renewed in mind and spirit.
We admit that in what we say and what we do we fail you.
When we are more ready to tell lies than speak the truth:
        Merciful God: **Forgive us our sins.**
When we are angry, and continue to bear a grudge:
        Merciful God: **Forgive us our sins.**
When we are not as honest as we lead others to believe:
        Merciful God: **Forgive us our sins.**

When we lose our temper and insult one another:
Merciful God: **Forgive us our sins.**
When we are selfish and unwilling to forgive:
Merciful God: **Forgive us our sins.**
Challenging God, we claim your forgiveness. Renew us by your Spirit, so that by what we are and what we do we may show that Jesus lives in us. We make our prayer in Jesus' name. **Amen.**

Activity
After the epistle, refer to the display of bags, which will have on them trade-marks, badges and branding signs of belonging and identity. Ask people about things which they wear which have a sense of identity; e.g. school tie, garment label, wedding ring – even a clerical collar! Ask for some items to be brought forward to the worship centre. Add to them a Christian sign, e.g. a cross or a fish, which shows commitment to the way of Christ.

Theme Prayer
Help us, loving God, not to be ashamed to show that we belong to you. Let our life together in the Spirit reveal your life and love at work in us, so that people around us may discover Jesus for themselves.

Thanksgiving
Holy God: For the truth about you revealed by Jesus,
We praise your holy name: **We offer you our thanks.**
For the gift of life which we can receive through faith in him,
We praise your holy name: **We offer you our thanks.**
For the seal of the Spirit in our lives marking us as yours,
We praise your holy name: **We offer you our thanks.**
For those whose lives have been changed by your Spirit,
We praise your holy name: **We offer you our thanks.**
For those with whom share we in the life of the church,
We praise your holy name: **We offer you our thanks.**
For those whose example has been influential in our lives,
We praise your holy name: **We offer you our thanks.**
For those whose generous, gentle and forgiving ways we value,
We praise your holy name: **We offer you our thanks.**
We thank you, God, that we are sealed by the Spirit and belong to you and each other, in the name of Jesus Christ. **Amen.**

Dismissal
Go as those who belong to the Spirit to live by the Spirit. **Amen.**

SUNDAY BETWEEN 14 AND 20

AUGUST   Twentieth Sunday in Ordinary Time

I Kings 2.10-12, 3.1–14; Psalm 111;
or Proverbs 9:1–6; Psalm 34:9–14.
Ephesians 5.15–20; John 6.51–58.

FILLED WITH THE SPIRIT

Worship Centre *Surround a loaf of bread and a cup of wine by a scattering of sheet music and hymn books.*

Approach
Come, let us worship.
God, you made us.
**We come, inspired by your Spirit,
with grateful hearts and ready minds, to hear your word.**

Adoration
'In the beginning, God created the heavens and the earth.'
God, you made the universe. Our minds cannot grasp the size of creation.
The universe began many million of years ago;
it is many million light-years big; it has many million galaxies and stars.
We are silent before the might and majesty of creation.
'In the beginning the Word already was ... through him all things came to be.'
God, you brought life into being. Life fills us with awe.
We wonder at the growth of an oak tree from a tiny acorn, at the liveliness of a cat, at the fragile beauty of a butterfly, at the power of our minds.
We are silent before the mystery and the wonder of life.
'In each of us the Spirit is seen to be at work.'
God, you are at work in each of us. Your amazing Spirit breathes within us, encouraging our talents and skills, giving us new powers and abilities, bringing new life, life eternal.
We are silent before the influence and the power of your presence within us.
Accept, God, our silent adoration, in the name of Jesus. **Amen.**

Confession
Accept, God, our silent confession.

Silence

Forgive us, God. **Fill us with your Spirit.**

You have put us in this universe.

We think how we spoil this earth you have given us to look after.

We poison the land. We foul the air. We pollute the sea.

Forgive us, God. **Fill us with your Spirit.**

You have given us life.

We think of how we fail to respect it.

We wipe out trees and plants; we destroy creatures great and small; we fight and hurt and kill each other.

Forgive us, God. **Fill us with your Spirit.**

You have breathed your life into us.

We think of how we do not let your Spirit work within us.

We give in to pride, we put our own interests first, we use our talents and abilities for our own ends.

Forgive us, God. **Fill us with your Spirit.**

God, forgive us and renew us. Help us to live as you would have us live. **Amen.**

Prayer of Praise

This should be led by two people – one holding up the loaf and the cup; the other holding up sheet music and hymn book.

A We rejoice, God, that because Jesus lives, we too can live.

B We rejoice that the Spirit fills our lives. We show you our love in words and music, raising our hearts and voices in praise.

A & B God, we give you our praise, through Jesus Christ. **Amen.**

Thanksgiving

Delighting in your Spirit, God, we come to thank you.

For your hovering Spirit, active in creation, giving shape and order, forming creatures and breathing in life.

In the name of Jesus. **Thank you, God.**

For your descending Spirit, active in time and space, revealed in Jesus your Son, in his life and ministry, in his death and resurrection.

In the name of Jesus. **Thank you, God.**

For your indwelling Spirit, active in our lives, giving us your truth, setting us free.

In the name of Jesus. **Thank you, God.**

For the wholeness of your Spirit, active in all the world, enabling us to understand our neighbours, and giving us power to do your will.

In the name of Jesus. **Thank you, God.**

Dismissal

Go in the Spirit, rejoicing in the name of our Lord Jesus. **Amen.**

SUNDAY BETWEEN 21 AND 27

AUGUST   Twenty-first Sunday in Ordinary Time

I Kings 8.22–30, 41–3; Psalm 84;
or Joshua 24.1–2a, 14–18; Psalm 34.15–22.
Ephesians 6.10–20; John 6.56–59.

PROTECTED AND EQUIPPED BY GOD

Worship Centre *Display in the worship centre the clothing and
equipment worn and used in an occupation or as part of an interest.
This will be a focus within the ministry of the word. If desired display
in other places further examples of protective clothing – e.g. light
waterproofs, wet-suit, safety helmet.*

Approach
Come, let us worship.
God, you made us.
**We come, prepared by the Spirit,
with grateful hearts and ready minds, to hear your word.**

Adoration
God, this is your day :
the day to recall the story of your energy exploding into creation.
God, this is your day :
the day to proclaim the good news of your energy in raising Jesus
from death.
God, this is your day :
the day to celebrate your energy poured into the friends of Jesus
enabling them to do amazing things.
God, this is your day:
this day on which we gather to be renewed by your activity, to
delight in your creative energy and to rejoice in your new life.
God, every day is your day: we worship and we praise you. **Amen.**

Time for Confession and Thanksgiving
allowing pauses for reflection
Let us look back over the days of the past week ...

Let us remember:
> the people we met – new and familiar;
> the places we went to – for work and for leisure;
> the way we spent our time.

Let us recall:
>the opportunities grasped and the opportunities missed;
>the difficulties faced and the difficulties avoided;
>the people we got on with and the people we gave up on.

We are sorry for the ways in which we have failed.
We ask for forgiveness.
We give thanks for all that is good in our lives.
We ask for support and guidance in the days ahead.
Say or sing 'St Patrick's Breastplate'
Christ be with me, Christ within me ...

Activity
Ask someone in the community with a particular occupation or interest to provide for the worship centre the protective clothing and equipment needed for that (e.g. paramedic, road sweeper, walker, health visitor). Before the reading of the Epistle, the various items are identified and explained, with the help of the person who uses them – perhaps in answer to questions. Explain that Paul was using familiar dress to picture the protection a Christian needed as a follower of Jesus. After the reading sing 'St Patrick's Breastplate' again.

Thanksgiving
We give thanks to God:
For people of faith who chose to serve God and made it possible for us to worship today.
Let us bless the Lord. **Thanks be to God.**
For people of trust who refused to compromise belief, and allowed God's Spirit to protect them.
Let us bless the Lord. **Thanks be to God.**
For people of courage who have ensured that the Good News was proclaimed boldly.
Let us bless the Lord. **Thanks be to God.**
For people of prayer who are signs for us of God's presence in the world.
Let us bless the Lord. **Thanks be to God.**
For people of hope who, through their life in the Spirit show us the way to God.
Let us bless the Lord. **Thanks be to God.**

Dismissal
Go in the strength of God and in the power of the Spirit, confident and equipped to stand firm for Christ. **Amen.**

SUNDAY BETWEEN 28 AUGUST AND 3 SEPTEMBER

Twenty-second Sunday in Ordinary Time

Song of Solomon 2.8–13; Psalm. 45.1–2, 6–9;
or Deuteronomy 4.1–2, 6–9; Psalm 15.
James 1.17–27; Mark 7.1–8, 14–15, 21–23.

WHAT MATTERS MOST

Worship Centre and Opening Words *A bowl of water stands to the side of a table, with a dishcloth, tea towel and an ordinary, dirty, large pot. This is then washed, inside and out, and placed centrally. As it is washed the following words can be used: the first section is read as the outside of the pot is washed; the second section as it is washed more thoroughly, particularly the inside; the third section as it is dried and placed centrally. This would be best done conversationally, either improvised or from memory, by the person washing the pot.*

If we wash the outside of a pot it looks clean.
It is good for appearances, but it is not enough.
Holy God, help us not to be satisfied with how we appear;
not to stop at thinking only about how other people see us.

To be truly clean, the inside must be washed.
Then what is put in the pot will not be made dirty, but will come out
fit to eat.
Holy God, help us to be clean inside, so that all that comes out of
us, all we are and all we say, might come from purity.

Here in worship we take our place before God;
we want to be clean inside, ready for prayer and the word of God.
Holy God, fill us, in our worship and in our lives;
let us be vessels for the glory of your love.

Confession and Absolution
Sometimes we say to someone 'I love you',
but then we scream and shout and behave as though we don't.
Sometimes we say, 'I want to make you happy',
but then we go away and do our own thing,
even though we know it makes someone sad.

Sometimes we say, 'You matter to me',
but we act as though other things matter more.

We are sorry for the times when we say one thing, but do another,
hurting our friends and hurting God.

Faithful God, when you say, 'You matter to me',
we know you mean it.

When you say, 'I love you',
we know it comes from the bottom of your heart.
When you say, 'I forgive you',
we know they are words we can trust,
because in Jesus you have put your word into action.
Thank you God for your unfailing love. **Amen.**

Offertory Prayer (*based on James 1.17-18*)
Blessed are you, God of all giving.
Blessed are you, Father of lights.
You are the source of every perfect gift, every gift from above.
You are the beginning of every generous act.
When the world turns there is day and there is night.
It casts its shadow upon itself.
But in the rolling ages of your creative act there is no shadow.
Your giving is faithful yet always new.
We could not give, had you not given first.
To you we come, the first-fruits of your creating.

Act of Commitment and Dismissal (*based on James 1.22–25*)
*Have small pieces of folded card ready for each person with short
Bible verses written on them. The verses give an instruction which
people can follow and obey during the coming week, for example:
Matthew 5.44, 6.33, 18.21–22; John 13.34; Romans 12.9–21; James
1.19b. Distribute them near the end of the service, possibly from the
clean pot in the worship centre. The following dismissal is then said
as the final act of the service while people hold up their cards.*
By the grace of God you have heard the living word.
God's Spirit is with us. **Thanks be to God.**
Now go out from here, but not as those who hear and forget.
Take the word of God in your hand and in your heart.
Put word into action.
God's Spirit is with us. **Thanks be to God.**
In the strength of that Spirit be doers of the word.
God's Spirit is with us. **Thanks be to God. Amen**

SUNDAY BETWEEN 4 AND 10
SEPTEMBER Twenty-third Sunday in Ordinary Time

Proverbs 22.1–2, 8-9, 22–23; Psalm 125;
or Isaiah 35.4–7a; Psalm 146.
James 2.1–17; Mark 7.24–37.

OPENING

Worship Centre *To develop the theme 'waters shall break forth in
the wilderness' lay out things which would be found in a desert (sand,
dry stone, dry wood, cactus) contrasted with running water (coloured
cellophane – blue, green and clear, or a small fountain powered by an
electric pump). Alternatively use two symbolic flower arrangements.*

Opening words

A   Where we feel dry, and our worship arid,
B   God, let your waters break out.
A   Where prayer has become monotonous,
B   God, may your refreshing streams bubble up.
A   Where boredom flattens your word in our ears,
B   God, open the flood gates of the Spirit.
A   In a world of death,
B   Give us living water to drink.

Imagining the Gospel Story
*In using this story and exercise particular sensitivity to the experi-
ence of people with hearing impairments in the congregation will be
needed.*
   Read the second half of the Gospel passage.
   *Ask people to sit in silence for about two minutes and imagine
   what it would be like for the deaf man before Jesus heals him. To
   end the silence say loudly and clearly, 'Ephphatha'.*
   *Play a tape, volume well turned up, of suitable sound effects (e.g.
   people's voices or bird song).*
   *Ask everyone to sing the two verses from 'O for a thousand
   tongues' beginning 'Jesus! the name that charms our fears' and
   'Hear him, ye deaf; his praise, ye dumb'.*

Petition
*The words 'Ephphatha. Be opened' would be effectively said by a
hidden voice.*

A	Where ears are shut, deaf to melody and the sounds of human speech, come and say
B	'Ephphatha. Be opened.'
A	Where ears are shut, deaf to protest and the cries of the poor, come and say
B	'Ephphatha. Be opened.'
A	Where tongues are mute, unable to shape words and songs, come and say
B	'Ephphatha. Be opened.'
A	Where tongues are mute, gagged by fear or lack of opportunity, come and say
B	'Ephphatha. Be opened.'
A	And where our hearts and minds are closed, where our prejudice and presumption impede the growth of others, come and say
B	'Ephphatha. Be opened.'
All	**Open our hearts, open our minds, open our ears, loose our tongues, to live the gospel with all our strength. Amen.**

Hymn *(based on Isaiah 35)*
Listen, for the stones are singing,
and the desert comes to birth
now the God of life sheds water,
spills it on the barren earth.

See the bloom of new creation,
fashioned by the Maker's hand,
breaks upon the weary desert –
blossoms fill the arid land.

Let the dusty, tired churches
hear the message, see God's power,
for the desert of our making
will not stop the Spirit's flower.

Where the blind perceive salvation,
where the lame can run the race,
where the dumb cannot keep silence,
see and know God's love and grace.

Now upon the Spirit's journey
we will walk the safe highway,
by our life and love affirming
our commitment to God's Day.
Andrew Lunn (possible tunes: Cross of Jesus; Halton Holgate)

SUNDAY BETWEEN 11 AND 17 SEPTEMBER

Twenty-fourth Sunday in Ordinary Time

Proverbs 1.20–33; Psalm 19 *or* Wisdom 7.26–8.1;
or Isaiah 50.4–9a; Psalm 116.1–9.
James 3.1–12; Mark 8.27–38.

UNASHAMED

Meditation and Confession (*based on Mark 8.27–38*)

A Jesus asked them, 'Who do you say that I am?' Peter answered him, 'You are the Messiah.'

B What am I ashamed of? I am ashamed of nothing. I am glad to be one of your followers; I believe you are God's chosen one; I will stand by you through thick and thin.

A Jesus began to teach them that the Son of Man must undergo great suffering. And Peter took him aside and began to rebuke him.

B What am I ashamed of? I am ashamed of powerlessness. I cannot accept a God who is not powerful; I don't want you to hang on a cross; I want an end to pain and suffering, not more of the same.

A And Jesus rebuked him and said, 'Get behind me Satan! For you are setting your mind not on divine things but on human things.'

B What am I ashamed of? I am ashamed of this rebuke. I don't want people to see my indignity; I want to hide my vulnerability and pain; I wish the ground would open up and swallow me.

A Jesus said to them, 'If any want to be a follower, let them deny themselves and take up their cross and follow me.'

B What am I ashamed of? I am ashamed of myself. I fall short of the high standards you set; I cannot live up to the self-giving you show us; I am ashamed of my weakness and incomprehension.

God, you are our challenger and adversary. We confess that we too are sometimes ashamed: ashamed of you and of ourselves. As we hear you say to us, 'Your sins are forgiven', lift us from shame and strengthen us to serve you in the strength of Jesus. **Amen.**

Dramatic Reflection (*for four readers*)

A What is a prophet?

B A prophet speaks for God.

C He says, 'This is what God wants from you.'

D	She says, 'This is what God will do.'
A	Prophets are in tune with God, and their words are true.
B+C	But their message is not always welcome.
A+D	People don't want to hear. They don't want to respond.
B	It challenges their vested interests.
C	It questions their lifestyle and their wealth.
D	It promises things they do not want.
A	It threatens them with doom they do not want to hear.
B+C	And sometimes the people become angry.
B+D	When the prophet speaks they put fingers in their ears.
A+C	They treat him with disdain and contempt.
B+D	She is put to shame.
A	But the prophet is still in tune with God.
C	He accepts the insults.
B	She sets her face like flint.
A	He does not turn back from what God has said.
A+C	So they beat him.
B+D	They spit on her.
C	They crucify him.

A	But God who vindicates is near.
B	Those whom the people call guilty, God calls true.
C	Those whom the people spit on, God washes clean.
D	Those whom the people slay, God raises up.
All	The prophet speaks for God.

Prayer of Commitment
The response after each section is
    Faithful God: **Let us stand firm with you.**
As an alternative response sing 'Stand, O stand firm'.
Other prayers relevant to local situations or international events
should replace these as needed.
Let us stand firm for the world's poor, unashamed to voice our protest, and to work for a fairer deal. **Response.**
Let us stand firm in our love for our children, unashamed to give them first place as Jesus did. **Response.**
Let us stand firm in our resolve to be a church open to everyone, unashamed to accept all who come through our doors. **Response.**
Let us stand firm against racism, unashamed to speak out against people with casual or violent prejudices. **Response.**
Let us stand firm for Jesus, unashamed to own him and name him. **Response.**

SUNDAY BETWEEN 18 AND 24 SEPTEMBER

Twenty-fifth Sunday in Ordinary Time

Proverbs 31.10–31; Psalm 1;
or Wisdom 1.16–2.1, 12–22; *or* Jeremiah 11.18–20; Psalm 54.
James 3.13–4.3, 7–8a; Mark 9.30–37.

AGAINST STATUS

Confession

A   I want to be better than my friend: I want to run faster than her.
I want to score more points:I want people to know I'm the best
Lord, have mercy. **Christ, have mercy. Lord, have mercy.**

B   I want to win the argument. I want everyone to hear what I think
I want to be heard more than I want to listen: I want the last word.
Lord, have mercy. **Christ, have mercy. Lord, have mercy.**

C   I want a world which goes *my* way.
I want trouble to happen in *other* countries.
I want to know nothing of the cost of my prosperity on others.
I want to be left in peace.
Lord, have mercy. **Christ, have mercy. Lord, have mercy.**

D   'But the wisdom from above is first pure, then peaceable, gentle,
willing to yield, full of mercy and good fruits, without a trace of
partiality or hypocrisy.'
Bless us with your wisdom. Deliver us from 'I want ...'
Renew us with words of forgiveness.

Silence

D   Jesus says, 'Your sins are forgiven'.

All **Thanks be to God. Amen.**

Dramatic Dialogue (*to follow the Gospel reading*)
*The exchange should rapidly become aggressive. The language
should be adapted and kept colloquial and informal.*

John   Bit tough, what he said to you the other day, Peter.

Peter   (*aggressive and defensive*) What d'you mean?

John   You haven't forgotten. Neither's anyone else. 'Get behind
me Satan,' he said. It's time you faced facts: you're not
number one any more.

Peter   He came to my boat first, John; called me first. Nothing
you say can change that.

Andrew   I'm with my brother; we were called together.

James   That doesn't give you any rights over us. We stick by him

	through thick and thin. 'Get behind me Satan.' Our loyalty has never been questioned like that.
Peter	Oh, that's really rich. Your loyalty never questioned! But who is it who's always left to be spokesman? Who is it that's always expected to speak up?
John	You just take it on yourself all the time. Don't start talking as though we forced it on you.
Judas	*(breaking in)* You all think you're so grand, don't you? Perhaps you need to look more carefully. Who does he really trust?
James	What d'you mean?
Judas	I mean when did he last give you anything of value to look after?
Peter	Don't try and pull that one on us. Just because you hold the purse strings doesn't make you anyone special.
Andrew	He's never cared that much about money anyway.
Judas	Just the kind of attitude you'd expect from a bunch of ill-educated fishermen.
John	Get knotted *(or use another appropriate colloquialism)*. *Enter Jesus. All look at him and freeze.*
Jesus	What is it you've been arguing about?

Thanksgiving

Living Christ, have you not come to us as a baby, small and helpless, not looking to be great, but to be like us?

Living Christ, you have reached out to us in generous love:

We reach out to you in thanks.

Have you not come to us as one who heals, reaching out to touch when others are frightened to get close, not looking to be clean and pure, but to be compassionate?

Living Christ, you have reached out to us in generous love:

We reach out to you in thanks.

Have you not come to us as a servant, thinking first of your disciples' tired feet, not looking to wear a crown, but to wrap a towel around your waist?

Living Christ, you have reached out to us in generous love:

We reach out to you in thanks.

Have you not come to us to be hurt and wounded, and even to die, not looking for easy glory, but waiting in the grave for God to act?

Living Christ, you have reached out to us in generous love:

We reach out to you in thanks.

Teach us to be those who in thankfulness welcome infants, embrace the poor, serve one another, and accept the wounds your service brings. For your love's sake. **Amen.**

SUNDAY BETWEEN
25 SEPTEMBER AND 1 OCTOBER

Twenty-sixth Sunday in Ordinary Time

Esther 7.1–6, 9–10, 9.20–22; Psalm 124;
or Numbers 11.4–6, 10–16, 24–29; Psalm 19.7–14.
James 5.13–20; Mark 9.38–50.

GOD OUTSIDE THE INNER CIRCLE

Worship Centre and Opening Words *A torn curtain is hung at
the front. It is most effective if the tear is from the top, nearly to
the bottom, but leaving a little intact, as though the tearing was in
progress.*
God will not be hemmed in; the separating curtain is torn in two.
God breaks out of our male images
   – will not be imprisoned by our church;
   – walks free from the chains of our demands.
God will appear wherever she chooses.

Confession, Absolution and Praise
*This is to be said by the whole congregation: the parts A and B then
indicate two halves of the congregation; the 'voice' should be from
the congregation, not from the front.*
God of the people, our God,
we confess before you and to one another all the wrong we have
   done,
all the wrong we have been part of.
As your people we try to keep you inside us,
when you have asked for words and actions.
As your church we try to control what people think of you,
when you are too big for us to imagine or comprehend.
As part of the world we try to take you over for political ends,
when you pour out your Spirit on the poor and powerless.
God of the people, our God, we are sorry for what we have done
   and been.
We place our trust in your challenging and forgiving love.
Silence

Voice	Proclaim with joy what God has done.
A	Hear the good news: God has forgiven you.
B	Praise God: holy three, redeeming one.
	Hear the good news: God has forgiven you.
A	Praise God: creating three, joyful one.

B	One God, author of the history of faith.
A	One God, the story-teller speaking to the world.
B	One God, the Word spoken to make us whole.
A	Praise God: joyful three, sanctifying one.
B	Praise God: forgiving three, holy one
A	by whose love our lives become one with the life of heaven. **Amen.**

Follow with a hymn of praise or the Gloria.

Meditation

Child A	Where is God? I can't find her.
Adult A	She wears disguises and hides her glory.
	I found her once in a young Hindu woman working in a women's refuge. Some people told me it couldn't be God, because the Christian God is the only true God, but I could only think of the love she showed.

Adult B	Where is God? I can't see him.
Child B	He hides in places you don't expect.
	I saw him once when an old man came into our church and began dancing at the front during a hymn. They said he'd had too much to drink, but I wish they hadn't shown him the door.

Adult A	Where is God? I can't feel him.
Adult B	He runs out to lose himself in the world.
	He touched me once when I was sad. I'd been to church that morning and it had left me cold; no help at all. But when my little girl came and gave me the biggest hug in the world, I knew God had just run by.

Child B	Where is God? I can't hear her.
Child A	She whispers and sings again and again.
	I've heard her early in the morning when the birds are singing; when my baby brother laughs and cries; when Nana says she loves me; when my friend said he wanted to make up after an argument. Mum says it's just my imagination, but I think God sings along with all of them.

Prayer for the Spirit

Spirit of God, come among us.
Spirit of God, transfigure the earth.
Go where you choose, roam free as the wind.
Draw into the commonwealth of God's love all manner of people.
Spirit of God, come among us.
Spirit of God, transfigure the earth. Amen.

SUNDAY BETWEEN 2 AND 8

OCTOBER   Twenty-seventh Sunday in Ordinary Time

Job 1.1, 2.1–10; Psalm 26; *or* Genesis 2.18–24; Psalm 8.
Hebrews 1.1–4, 2.5–12; Mark 10.2–16.

NAMING CHILDREN IN THE CHURCH

Worship Centre *An outline drawing of a church building, displayed so that it can be seen by everyone, but at a height which anyone present can reach.*

Call to Worship
Psalm 8.1

Confession
When the church prefers to worship success,
rather than see God's greatness in the small:
> Then will Jesus say: **Let the children come.**
When the church wants to be important, too busy for laughter:
> Then will Jesus say: **Let the children come.**
When the church seeks to silence the voices of its children,
finding the enthusiasm of young people a nuisance:
> Then will Jesus say: **Let the children come.**
When the church is afraid of people who are sad,
because it cannot provide all the answers:
> Then will Jesus say: **Let the children come.**
When the church cannot bear to be adventurous,
choosing to play safe rather than risking mistakes:
> Then will Jesus say: **Let the children come.**
When the church is eager to speak, so it forgets the call to listen:
> Then will Jesus say: **Let the children come.**
Silence
God of hope, you promise that the gate of mercy will stand open:
Welcome us into your kingdom through Jesus Christ our Lord.

Ministry of the Word *(to follow the Bible readings)*
Voice A (A Woman) I need a name. The 'wife of Job' is simply not enough. I deserve more than being slapped into silence by a pious patriarch. I need a name.
I am more than simply the mother of children – though God's heavenly haggle has meant that I am less than that. I need a name.
I am Woman of the Bible, barren, battered, banished, birth-giver.

104

God of the glorious name: cherish history's nameless women, caress them into full humanity. Meet me again in the garden, wipe away my tears, dare to know me as your own.

Leader: Let us, with her, declare:

I will proclaim your name to my brothers and sisters.
In the midst of the congregation I will praise you.

Voice B (A Child) I need a name. 'Child of Job' is not enough. My life deserves more than that, more than being the object of a divine experiment. I need a name.

I felt, I loved; therefore I was. I will not be just an unknown victim. I need a name.

I am Child of the Bible, spoiled, sinned against, sent away, sacrificed. God of the glorious name: bend down to history's nameless children, guide them with reins of love.

Let me come to you, lift me in your arms, call me into your kingdom.

Leader: Let us with God's children declare:

I will proclaim your name to my brothers and sisters.
In the midst of the congregation I will praise you.

Voice C (A Man) I need a name. I thought I had one. Job, or maybe Adam, the first human being. But when God drew woman out of man, was a part of my humanity removed?

I need to know who I am. What am I, that God is mindful of me? Man of the Bible, pained, perplexed. Call me by name. I am me.

God of the glorious name: what do you want me for: slave, workman or friend? Remember me, your creature, when you draw the bounds of your kingdom.

Leader: Let us, with him, declare:

I will proclaim your name to my brothers and sisters,
In the midst of the congregation I will praise you.

Voice D (Jesus) I have a name. It is Jesus, Son of God, yet bone of your bone, flesh of your flesh. I call all humankind my brothers and sisters, I have shared with them my name.

I have no wife – yet every woman is known to me, by name.

I have no son or daughter – yet each child tells of God's glory.

I am man's pattern – though by men rejected.

I hung alone, and in my solitude became the pioneer of your salvation.

Leader: Let us, children and women and men together, declare:

I will proclaim your name to my brothers and sisters,
In the midst of the congregation I will praise you.

Action

Each person writes the name they are called by on a 'Post-it' note and places it on the outline of the church at the worship centre.

SUNDAY BETWEEN 9 AND 15 OCTOBER
Twenty-eighth Sunday in Ordinary Time

Job 23.1–9, 16–17; Psalm 22.1–5;
or Amos 5.6–7, 10–15; Psalm 90.12–17.
Hebrews 4.12–16; Mark 10.17–31.

PLAYING HIDE-AND-SEEK WITH GOD

Preparation *Hide from sight some of the objects which are usually in the church building and which people might say give a sense of the sacredness e.g. candle, chalice, Bible, cross.*

Call to Worship
Satisfy us at daybreak with your steadfast love, that we may sing for joy and be glad all our days *(Psalm 90.14)*.

Reflection and Prayer
Rabbi Baruch's grandson was upset because his friend couldn't be bothered to look for him when they played hide-and-seek. His grandfather, his eyes full of tears, told him that God says the same thing: 'I hide, but no one wants to seek me' *(Martin Buber)*.

A If only I could vanish from God in darkness.
B No creature is hidden before God.
A The Almighty terrifies me, God has made my heart faint.
B Before God's eyes all are naked and exposed.
A The word of God is sharper than a sword.
B Go sell all you own, and give the money to the poor.
A I am fearful of meeting God
B Yet in God alone is healing and delight.
A What must I do to inherit eternal life?
B Seek good and not evil, that you may live, and that the Lord may be with you.
A O that I knew where I might find God! If I go forward, God is not there. If I go backwards, I cannot find God. On the left, God hides: I look right, and I cannot see God!
B Yet we have a great high priest, who has passed through the heavens, who can sympathize with our weakness.
A My God, my God, why have you forsaken me?
B My God, my God, why have you forsaken me?
Silence and Pause
A & B We have a great high priest who has passed through the

heavens, Jesus the Son of God. So let us approach God with
boldness that we may receive mercy and find grace.

Prayer of Thanksgiving
Thank you God.
You enjoy the company of your human playmates.
Sometimes the games you play seem a bit one sided and unfair.
'The first will be last and the last will be first' really gets me.
I'm frightened of it and I don't want to play it too often.
Yet thank you God. **You look upon me and love me.**
Thank you God. You delight in games of hide-and-seek.
I do too, just as long as I can be the one who hides.
I know you will search for me, but am I as eager to seek for you?
Sometimes it feels all too easy to want to give up the quest.
So thank you God. **You look upon me and love me.**
Thank you God. You have never been any good at Monopoly.
You want to be on our side all the time, rather than play against us.
People get annoyed with you because you would rather go bankrupt
    than own Mayfair.
But the extravagance of your love means that there are no losers.
I will thank you God. **You look upon me and love me.**
I have always puzzled at your teasing riddles, God.
You know some great posers!
The one about the camel and the eye of a needle really got the
    learned scholars going.
They started looking all over Jerusalem for a narrow gate
The idea that you might be telling a joke. That's simply awesome!
Wow, thank you God. **You look upon me and love me.**
But I know your favourite game, God, it's treasure hunting.
I enjoy it, but your idea of treasure feels so different from mine.
You tell me of treasure that is to be stored up for me in heaven.
I will have to solve so many clues before I discover that hoard.
Yet I know you will always look upon me and love me.
Thank you God. **You look upon me and love me.**

Offering and Prayer
*When the collection is to be brought up, first get people to identify
which objects are missing in the church, and then to find them. Bring
them forward with the collection.*

Blessing
May the love of God, as father and mother, reach out to hold you.
May the Christ of God always laugh and cry with you.
And may the Spirit captivate you with the beauty of holiness.

SUNDAY BETWEEN 16 AND 22
OCTOBER Twenty-ninth Sunday in Ordinary Time

Job 38.1–7 (34–41); Psalm 104.1–9, 24, 35c;
or Isaiah 53.4–12; Psalm 91.9–16.
Hebrews 5.1–10; Mark 10.35–45.

DIFFICULT QUESTIONS

Worship Centre *Display a large picture, poster or a collage to show the power and contradictions of natural phenomena (e.g. a volcano erupting, a natural disaster – avalanche, flood, storm – or a view of the world taken from space).*

Call to Worship *Psalm 104.24*

Prayer of Adoration and Confession
If only we had been there when the earth was born:
perhaps we would have seen more clearly
how precious is our world, how fragile and irreplaceable.
We might have cherished it better and loved it more.
If only we had been there –
when the morning stars sang together,
and the holy ones shouted for joy.
If only we had been there
when the vast cathedral of the skies first soared aloft:
perhaps the music of the stars
would have soothed our spirits,
and played their harmonies into the lyrics of our lives.
We too might have learned by heart the great psalm of peace.
If only we had been there –
when the morning stars sang together,
and the holy ones shouted for joy.
If only we had been there when people could meet God
face to face, in garden or in whirlwind:
perhaps it would have been easier to live with questions,
knowing God didn't want us to stop asking them.
We might have understood they can't all be answered – at least this
side of eternity.
If only we had been there –
when the morning stars sang together,
and the holy ones shouted for joy.
If only we had been there,

when the lamb of God was offered before the world's foundation:
perhaps we would have grasped God's perfect pattern,
how love and sacrifice are woven into the fabric of the universe.
We might have learned obedience, following the servant Son.
If only we had been there –
when the morning stars sang together,
and the holy ones shouted for joy.

Meditation *(to be used at a point after the readings)*
I'm telling you now, God, I've got rather a lot of questions.
I expect you to answer them.
Some of them are very important – to me at least.
After all, I'm the most important one here, at least in my own eyes.
So naturally I reckon that I'll get the best seat going – in heaven,
    even if not on earth.
What? You've got a question for me first? What do you mean about
    drinking from cups?
The same cup as you? I don't understand.
It's not fair to ask me things that I can't be expected to grasp.
No, of course I wasn't there when you created the world!
That question is out of order: it's simply not fair!
But now you say that no question you ask can be out of order since
    you are responsible for the order of the universe.
Really, you are making up the rules of this quiz as you go along!
If I might get a word in, what I want to ask is ...
Why do good people suffer?
I don't have a problem about the wicked – it's what they deserve.
But there are plenty of good people around (and without wanting to
    sound too big-headed – I include myself) who don't seem to have
    life going all their own way.
You're telling me that we're not meant to have it all our own way?
Can't you do something about that?
Sorry, I didn't quite catch that: did you say that you yourself found
    life painful enough? That can't be right.
I can't hear you properly; this whirlwind makes too much noise.
Perhaps I'd better shut up.
But I think I'm beginning to see ...

Dismissal
May the singing of the stars of heaven echo in our hearts.
May the wounds of the Man of Sorrows nourish our souls.
And may the whirling and tempestuous Spirit of God breathe new
    life upon our faces, now and always. **Amen**

SUNDAY BETWEEN 23 AND 29 OCTOBER Thirtieth Sunday in Ordinary Time

Job 42.1–6, 10–17; Psalm 34.1–8, 19–22;
or Jeremiah 31.7–9; Psalm 126.
Hebrews 7.23–28; Mark 10.46–52.

ONE WORLD, FOR ALL

Worship Centre *Display utensils containing water, to reflect its use in both the developing and the developed world, e.g. glass jug, bottled water, bucket, hosepipe.*

Call to Worship
Those who sow in tears, shall reap with shouts of joy *(Psalm 126).*
Pause
'You have no tears? Buy tears from the poor. You have no sadness?
Call those suffering poverty to moan with you. If your heart is hard and has neither sadness nor tears, with alms invite the needy to weep with you' *(Jacob of Saroug).*

Prayer of adoration
A The shouts are too loud
   they deafen my ears.
   War, famine, destruction, death –
   the sufferings of the world glide past my eyes.
   I have heard too much, I have seen too much: I do not care.
B The people are too many,
   they blur together in my imagination,
   races, colours, faiths, languages,
   in shifting kaleidoscopes make me dizzy.
   I have seen too much, I have heard too much: I do not care.
A But you, O God,
   you stand in the middle of the world's sadness,
   and the people who suffer are no longer faceless,
   for you have given them your own face.
   And I shall proclaim: **I had heard, but now I see.**
B For you, O God,
   you are the still point round which everything revolves,
   in you both light and shadow are balanced:
   in colours of rainbow hope you paint our many-peopled world.
   And I shall proclaim: **I had heard but now I see.**

Prayer of Confession
When we are deaf to the cries of those in need, because they are too painful for us to hear:
Jesus, son of David, have mercy on us.

When we feel embarrassed by extravagant gestures of faith, because they challenge our complacency:
Jesus, son of David, have mercy on us.

When we find it difficult to admit we might have been wrong, because we cling to our need to be right:
Jesus, son of David, have mercy on us.

When our eyes remain hard and dry, because we have not learned to weep:
Jesus, son of David, have mercy on us.

When following Jesus feels too great a risk, and we choose to stand aside:
Jesus, son of David, have mercy on us.

'Take heart: get up, God is calling you.'
Jesus says: 'Your faith has made you well.'
Amen.

Ministry of the Word
In Hebrew (as in other Semitic languages) the word used for 'the eye' and for a 'spring of water' is identical – 'Ein. Eyes are the source or 'spring' of tears. Tears are therapeutic, they can lead to reconciliation and even resurrection (see e.g. Genesis 45.1–4, John 11.35, 20.11). Can our tears shed in empathy and sympathy help to give life to our world?
Follow this reflection with prayers about the use of water, and/or use the meditation and reflection in the material in this book for Lent 1 (pp.38–9).

Dismissal
Cast off the cloaks that cling so heavily upon you.
Open your eyes and look upon the world with new vision,
and follow Jesus in the way of God,
rejoicing in faith and hope and love.

1 NOVEMBER

All Saints

Wisdom of Solomon 3.1–9 *or* Isaiah 25.6–9;
Psalm 21; Revelation 21.1–6a; John 11.32–44.

SAINTS

Worship Centre *Display emblems representing different saints e.g. the four evangelists, or the ten contemporary martyrs whose statues stand on the west front of Westminster Abbey. Alternatively use emblems for groups of saints: a church building for founders of churches; a crown for royalty; the mitre or pastoral staff for bishops, abbots or abbesses; a palm or sword for martyrs; a pen and book for learned people. Think of emblems to represent local people who could be called saints. Use the emblems as a visual focus for intercessory prayer.*

Litany of Modern Saints
Ask different people sitting among the congregation to read the groups of names.
Let us give thanks for all God's saints:
Saints of God, faithful to the end:
Martyrs of Christ, who point us to God.
A Protesting against injustice, standing with the poor:
 Oscar Romero, Martin Luther King, Janani Luwum, Elizabeth of Hesse-Darmstadt.
Saints of God, faithful to the end:
Martyrs of Christ, who point us to God.
B Giving all for others, loving to the end:
 Maximilian Kolbe, Esther John, Dietrich Bonhoeffer.
Saints of God, faithful to the end:
Martyrs of Christ, who point us to God.
C Standing firm in faith, standing firm for Christ:
 Manche Masemola, Lucian Tapiedi, Wang Zhiming.
Saints of God, faithful to the end:
Martyrs of Christ, who point us to God.

Prayer of Praise (*based on Revelation 21.1–6a*)
God, Alpha and Omega, beginning and end:
For beginning the world you made for us, calling its life into being,
for breathing your breath upon it;

God, beginning and end, we praise you:
From our beginning to our end, we praise you.
For the ending of this world when your time is right, for bringing all
things to completion,
for finishing what you began;
God, beginning and end, we praise you:
From our beginning to our end, we praise you.
For beginning each of us in the womb, calling us by name,
for breathing your Spirit of life into us;
God, beginning and end, we praise you:
From our beginning to our end, we praise you.
For the ending of this life you have given us, for the sleep of death,
and the day of resurrection;
God, beginning and end, we praise you:
From our beginning to our end, we praise you.
For the beginning of a new heaven and a new earth,
a place for your people to live with you forever;
God, beginning and end, we praise you:
From our beginning to our end, we praise you.
For the ending of death and its threatening power,
for an end to crying, mourning and pain, when you will wipe all
tears away;
God, beginning and end, we praise you:
From our beginning to our end, we praise you.
For new beginning,
for the resurrection life of Jesus, the hope of all your people;
God, beginning and end, we praise you:
From our beginning to our end, we praise you.

Prayer of Thanksgiving and Petition
God you alone are holy,
but today we thank you for people who have, through your grace,
    lived holy lives:
not through doing special deeds but simply by being faithful,
not by living outside the world, but by serving you in it,
not by setting themselves above others, but by seeing you in them,
not by thinking they were saints, but by knowing they had sinned in
    your eyes.
(Especially we thank you for ...)
Help us to follow the example of your saints,
to stand firm in our faith, to see and serve you in the world
and to live in humility and trust all the days you give us. **Amen.**

SUNDAY BETWEEN 30 OCTOBER AND 5 NOVEMBER

Thirty-first Sunday in Ordinary Time

Ruth 1.1–18; Psalm 146;
or Deuteronomy 6.1–9; Psalm 119.1–8.
Hebrews 9.11–14; Mark 12.28–34.

GOD'S LAW OF LOVE

Worship Focus *Write out the summary of the law (Mark 12.29–31a) on large sheets of paper. Attach them to the doors of the church and in a central position in the worship area.*

Preparation for Worship *Give out photocopied prayer cards with the prayer of approach on as people come into worship. Suggest they use them in preparation for worship and at home when they go to bed and when they rise.*

Prayer of Approach
God, the one eternal God
you are my God and I love you.
With the warmth of my heart, I love you.
With the depth of my soul, I love you.
With the reasoning of my mind, I love you.
With the strength of my body, I love you.
God come to me in waking and sleep,
in neighbour and stranger,
in word and silence,
now and always. **Amen.**

Litany

All	**Lord teach us your ways.**
	Remind us of your commandments.
	Write them on our hearts, write them on our hands.
Women	Hear, men of God; the Lord our God is the one Lord.
Men	We will love God with all our hearts.
	Hear, women of God; the Lord our God is the one Lord.
Women	We will love God with all our minds and our strength.
	Hear, children of God; the Lord our God is the one Lord.
Children	We will love God with all that we are.
	Hear, people of God; the Lord our God is the one Lord.

All	**Lord teach us your ways.**
	Remind us of your commandments.
Men	For your commandments lead to life.
Women	Life eternal, life everlasting.
Children	Write them on our hearts.
Men	Write them on our hands.
Women	Your commandments surround us night and day.
Children	When we lie down to sleep and when we wake up.
All	**When we work and when we play,**
	Help us to remember them.
Children	Lord teach us your ways.
Women	Remind us of your commandments.
Men	Write them on our hearts.
Women	Write them on our hands.
Children	Lord, remind us of your commandments.
All	**Teach us to love.**

Prayer of Thanksgiving

God of compassion, lover of all,
thank you for the people who live your love in the world;
gentle people who work with the broken and vulnerable,
sharing their pain, helping them to trust again.
You who live God's love, hear the words of Jesus:
You are not far from the kingdom of God.

God of compassion, lover of all,
thank you for the people who live your love in the world;
caring people who work with the sick and the dying,
soothing their distress, giving them dignity.
You who live God's love, hear the words of Jesus:
You are not far from the kingdom of God.

God of compassion, lover of all,
thank you for the people who live your love in the world;
those who love justice, who search for the truth,
freeing the oppressed, giving a voice to the poor.
You who live God's love, hear the words of Jesus:
You are not far from the kingdom of God.

God of compassion, lover of all,
we are your people, called to live your love in the world;
in our gentleness and caring,
in our passion for justice and truth,
whenever we live your love, let us hear the words of Jesus:
You are not far from the kingdom of God.

SUNDAY BETWEEN 6 AND 12 NOVEMBER

Thirty-second Sunday in Ordinary Time

Ruth 3.1–5, 4.13–17; Psalm 127;
or I Kings 17.8–16; Psalm 146.
Hebrews 9.24–28; Mark 12.38–44.

THE GENEROSITY WHICH GIVES EVERYTHING

Worship Centre Either *use a large jar or similar container full of flour laid on its side with flour spilling out and a bottle of cooking oil* or *use two collection plates, one overflowing with bank notes, the other with two small coins.*

Story Idea *'Tonio's Gift' (see p.127).*

Prayer of Approach
Holy God, Creator of all,
from nothing you made a world of beauty
and from the dust you made all humanity.
Today from the poverty of our worship
and the smallness of our faith,
create for your glory
praise which overflows, abundant thanksgiving.
and hearts filled with your Spirit. **Amen.**

Meditation (*based on Mark 12.41–44*)
Ideally this meditation should follow the Gospel reading. It should be taken quite slowly with pauses which allow people plenty of time for thought and prayer especially where indicated by a series of dots.

Spend a moment thinking about the things you own, your possessions.
Which is the most important of all of them? Which means most to you …?
Now think about why that object means so much. Is it because of material value, sentimental value, because of its beauty, because it has spiritual value?
Now imagine what it would be like to give that object away. Who would you be prepared to give it to? A relation, a friend, a charity?
What thoughts and feelings do you have …?

116

In your imagination you decide to give your gift to charity.
When you have given it you notice that Jesus is there and he has
seen you.
What does Jesus say to you ...? What do you say to him ...?
How do Jesus' words make you feel? ...
How do you feel now about your valued object?

Selfless God,
fill our hearts with gratitude for all the gifts you give to us;
help us use them as Jesus would;
take away our greed and fill us with generosity
to share your good gifts with all. Amen.

Reflective Prayer
The widow of Zarephath, with a handful of flour and a drop of oil
fed the prophet of God before her child and herself.
> God, teach us the joy of hospitality,
> which welcomes friend and stranger, neighbour and enemy,
> and finds you feasting among us.

The widow of Jerusalem, with a couple of tiny coins
offered to God her love, her worship and all she had.
> God, teach us the joy of giving freely,
> which counts nothing as ours by right, but willingly shares,
> and finds you sharing with us.

Faithful widows, by their generosity supporting the work of God
gave what they had in spite of ridicule and rejection.
> God, teach us the joy of integrity,
> which values every offering, is open-hearted in honesty,
> and finds your truth within us.

Lord Jesus Christ, with your whole being
you sacrificed yourself for your love of us.
Teach us the joy of giving ourselves to you,
so that we yearn for your presence, long for your salvation,
and find you living in us. **Amen.**

Prayer at the Dismissal
Out of your giving, Generous God,
we make our offering.
We offer you, for your fulfilling,
praise which overflows,
abundant thanksgiving
and hearts filled with your Spirit. **Amen.**

SUNDAY BETWEEN 13 AND 19 NOVEMBER

Thirty-third Sunday in Ordinary Time

I Samuel 1.4–20; I Samuel 2.1–10;
or Daniel 12:1–3; Psalm 16.
Hebrews 10.11–25; Mark 13.1–8.

BIRTH PANGS AND END TIMES

Worship Centre *A base for building a tower of cardboard boxes.*

Call to Worship

Good morning!	**Good morning!**
It's a good day!	**It is God's day!**
God's day is coming!	**God's new day waits to be born!**

Gospel Activity *(following the Gospel reading)*
Invite people to pick up a cardboard box and to write on one side words that represent power and destruction in the world:'Poverty', 'Hunger', 'Wealth', 'Abuse', 'Unemployment', 'Selfishness', 'Cruelty' etc. The response in bold may be said as written or replaced by a sung phrase (e.g. the first verse of 'Come Lord Jesus, Come' or an 'Amen').

The disciples said to Jesus, 'Tell us, when will this be, and what will be the sign that all these things are about to be accomplished?'
Come Lord Jesus, come: **Amen, amen, alleluia, amen.**

'Look, Teacher, what large stones! What large buildings!'
Jesus said, 'Do you see these great buildings? Not one stone will be left here upon another; all will be thrown down.'
Come Lord Jesus, come: **Amen, amen, alleluia, amen.**

Jesus said, 'Beware that no one leads you astray. Many will come in my name and say, "I am he!" and they will lead many astray.'
Come Lord Jesus, come: **Amen, amen, alleluia, amen.**

Jesus said, '... nation will rise against nation, and kingdom against kingdom; there will be earthquakes in various places; there will be famines. These are but the beginning of the birth pangs.'
Come Lord Jesus, come: **Amen, amen, alleluia, amen.**

Responsive Affirmation (*Song of Hannah, I Samuel 2.1–10 and Psalm 113. To be read by three female voices, of different ages. Take the tower down in stages between the verses and at the end.*)

A   Praise the Lord, you servants of the Lord!
        Praise the name of the Lord!
        In the Lord I can hold my head up high,
        I can laugh at all God's enemies.
The Lord has filled my heart with joy: I rejoice in God's salvation.

        Those who boast of their power are left without strength.
        Those counted feeble are given new energy.
        Those who had plenty have to beg for dry bread
        while the hungry ones will be filled by God's goodness.
The Lord has filled my heart with joy: I rejoice in God's salvation.

B   In God's hand are life and death.
        God sends down to the grave and raises to life.
        In God's hand are poverty and wealth.
        The proud are set aside and the humble lifted up.
The Lord has filled my heart with joy: I rejoice in God's salvation.

        The Lord lifts up the weak from the dust.
        The Lord raises the poor from misery.
        There is no one to set beside our God.
        In God is our rock and our salvation.
The Lord has filled my heart with joy: I rejoice in God's salvation.

C   There is no one to set beside God, our Saviour.
        None so holy as the Lord!
        The foundations of the world are established by God.
        On them the whole world is built.
The Lord has filled my heart with joy: I rejoice in God's salvation.

        When the heavens are filled with thunder
        Those who rebel against God will be afraid.
        The Lord is the judge over all the earth.
        May the Lord be praised for ever!
        The Lord has filled my heart with joy:
A,B,C   We rejoice in God's salvation.

Leaving Song
'Behold, behold I make all things new' sung repeatedly as people leave.

SUNDAY BETWEEN 20 AND 26 NOVEMBER
Sunday before Advent

II Samuel 23.1–7; Psalm 93.13–14;
or Daniel 7.9–10; Psalm 132.1–12 (13–18).
Revelation 1.4b–8; John 18.33–37.

CHRIST THE KING

Worship Centre *As an acting out of a call to worship, create the worship centre. Ask people to process forward with gold candles, or candles in gold-coloured holders, a golden crown, and a handful of glass nuggets representing jewels, all to be placed on a gold cloth (already in place). Finally light the candles.*

Acclamations of Praise *(from Revelation 1.4b–8, 7.12)*
'Grace to you and peace from him who is and who was and who is to come.'
All praise to you, God of all, for your blessing upon us now, for your blessing upon us in what has been and for the gifts of grace and peace you wait to give us.
'To him who loves us and freed us from our sins by his blood,
and made us to be a kingdom, priests serving his God and Father,
to him be glory and dominion forever and ever.'
All praise to you, Jesus Christ, for your great love for us, for giving yourself for us, and for bringing us back to the Father.
'Look! He is coming with the clouds; every eye will see him.'
Lord Jesus, we look in expectant hope to the day of your great glory, and wait with eager breath to join with all creation in your praise.
' "I am the Alpha and the Omega," says the Lord God,
who is and who was and who is to come, the Almighty.'
'Amen! Blessing and glory and wisdom and thanksgiving and honour and power and might be to our God forever and ever! Amen.'

Confession *(reader B takes the part of Jesus)*
A   Lord Jesus, you are our King.
B   It is you who say that I am,
        for lies are still told, people deceived,
        truth is not lived in word and deed.
        My kingdom does not belong to this world.
        My kingdom comes where truth is heard.

Where truth is told and truth is done
my kingdom has come, life in heaven begun.

A   Lord Jesus you are our King.

B   It is you who say that I am,
        for there is hypocrisy still, people deceived,
        truth is not lived in word and deed.
     My kingdom does not belong to this world.
     My kingdom comes where truth is heard.
   Where truth is told and truth is done
   my kingdom has come, life in heaven begun.

A   Lord Jesus you are our King.

B   It is you who say that I am,
        for truth is still compromised, people deceived,
        truth is not lived in word and deed.
     My kingdom does not belong to this world.
     My kingdom comes where truth is heard.
   Where truth is told and truth is done
   my kingdom has come, life in heaven begun.

Silence

A   Lord Jesus we want you to be our King
   but we have lied and denied you, evaded and deceived,
     and not lived the truth in word and deed.
     Forgive us our sin, help us to hear
     the truth you proclaim to live without fear.
   So may your kingdom come in all we say and do,
   life in heaven begun, your people made new.

Collect

Stir up your power, Lord Jesus, and free us from our sins:
In your grace and mercy bring us to the fullness of your salvation:
for you are alive and reign for ever and ever. **Amen.**

Prayer at the Dismissal (*using Daniel 7.9–10*)
God of all, from our beginning to our end you are our God.
     From our beginning to our end we will praise you!
God, Ancient in Years, we attend upon you.
God, Ancient in Years, bring us to your throne of fire.
     With purifying fire cleanse us,
     with the heat of fire warm our hearts,
     with the power of fire strengthen us to serve you.
God, Ancient in Years, take your seat among us. **Amen.**

MOTHERING SUNDAY

Fourth Sunday in Lent

THE JOYS AND PAINS OF LOVING

Worship Centre *Make a crown of thorns by binding blackberry canes into a circle along with prunings from rose bushes. Put in a central place. Have some roses ready.*

Prayer of Approach
As for the Fourth Sunday in Lent (pp.44–5)

Confession
As for Fourth Sunday in Lent (pp.44–5)

Ministry of the Word
While quiet music is played pass the roses around. Encourage people to look at them carefully. Ask the last people to hold on to them while thoughts are shared (about the contrast of beauty and thorns). Have someone speak briefly about the joy and pain of parenthood. Focus also on the joy and pain of God as loving father and mother.

Song
'Christ had a garden' (*Oxford Book of Carols*) sung by soloist if possible.

Action
Ask those holding the roses to bring them forward. Cut away part of the stems and place the roses in the crown of thorns.

Petition
Loving Mother God,
We pray for mothers:
– mothers who are often kind, generous and self-sacrificing
– mothers who are often tired, short-tempered and selfish.
We pray for parents:
– parents who give up a great deal for their children
– parents who find it hard to be giving of themselves all the time.
We pray for families:
– families where relationships are rich and fulfilling
– families where relationships are stretched to breaking point.

Loving Father God,
You know both the pain and the joy of parenthood.
Out of your great love you have given us life,
together with your Son, Jesus.

Loving Mother and Father God,
We bring you our pain and joy.
We bring you our love.

Song 'God, you hold me like a mother'

Appendix 1: Supplementary Material

Epiphany

Epiphany cake (*Galette des Rois*) – an alternative idea.
Use a basic madeira cake recipe. Add grated lemon rind, one dried bean, one dried pea and, maybe, some trinkets. Decorate it with stars, crowns or three kings. The one who finds the bean is the king, the one who finds the pea is queen.

Sixth Sunday in Ordinary Time

Response for prayers of intercession and offering.

Russian Orthodox Liturgy

Re – mem – ber your ser – vants, Lord,

when you come in to your king - dom.

Palm Sunday

Making crosses for Palm Sunday
Palm leaves can be obtained from SPCK and other outlets. If you are unable to obtain palm, the crosses may be made from long, thin strips of paper.
*1   Split in half lengthwise
*2-4 See diagram
*5-9 See diagram

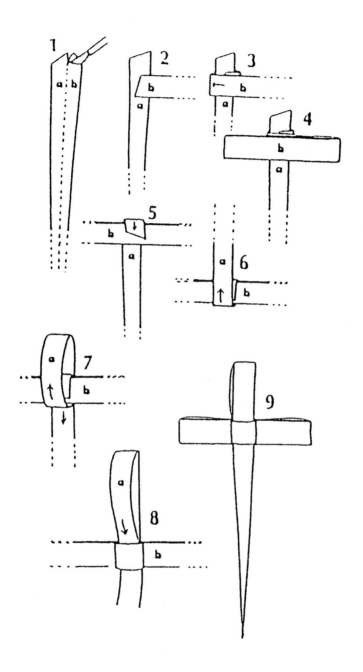

Easter Day

The Dramatised Bible, Harper Collins 1989

Second Sunday of Easter

Easter Antiphon

All Saints

Penguin Dictionary of Saints ed Donald Attwater, Penguin 1983

Pictures of the emblems of the four evangelists can be found in *The
Lindisfarne Gospels* by Janet Backhouse, Phaidon Press 1987, and on the
front covers of Pelican Gospel Commentaries.

Ten recent martyrs whose statues stand on the west front of Westminster
Abbey:

Oscar Romero – Archbishop of San Salvador who identified with the poor
and persecuted and pleaded their cause. He was isolated both inside and
outside the church. In March 1980 he was shot dead while celebrating Mass.

Martin Luther King – ordained minister inspired by his Christian faith to
fight for black civil rights using non-violent methods. Shot in Memphis in
1964, aged 39.

Janani Luwum – Archbishop of Uganda, killed by Idi Amin in 1976 when he protested about the violence of the security services.

Elizabeth of Hesse-Darmstadt – founder of the Mary and Martha home in Moscow, becoming with others the Sisters of Love and Charity engaged in work of prayer and charity. Elizabeth was arrested and killed with hundreds of other nuns and priests by the Bolsheviks after the 1917 revolution.

Maximilian Kolbe – who died in Auschwitz-Birkenau in 1941, giving his life to save a fellow prisoner.

Esther John – Born as Qamar Zia in a Muslim family in India, she attended a Christian school, later developing her faith in secret following a family move to Pakistan. Fleeing a Muslim marriage she changed her name to Esther John and evangelized in the villages around Chichawatni, teaching women to read and working with them in the fields. In 1960 she was found murdered in her bed.

Dietrich Bonhoeffer – a Lutheran pastor who saw the dangers of Nazism and tried to warn the German Protestant churches. As war loomed he chose to return to Germany. He was arrested in March 1943 for resistance activities and executed in April 1945.

Manche Masemola – a 14-year-old South African girl killed by her parents in 1928 because she would not give up her Christian faith.

Lucian Tapiedi – born in 1921 in Taupota, Papua New Guinea. A Christian and a teacher killed while trying to escape from the Japanese with a group of missionaries. Later his murderer converted to Christianity and built a church in memory of Tapiedi.

Wang Zhiming – Pastor in Wuding county, in Yunnan region of China, during the Cultural Revolution (1966–76), when Christians met in secret. Wang Zhiming was arrested in May 1969 and executed in 1973 at a mass rally of more than 10,000 people organized by the Red Guard.

Thirty-second Sunday in Ordinary Time

Five-year-old Tonio was chosen to be the youngest shepherd in the Nativity play. The children were asked to bring a present for the babe in the manger. Tonio, whose family was very poor, brought his most precious possession, a piece of wood, worn smooth with handling. It was his only toy, which he had kept hidden and played with in secret, otherwise it would have been taken from him and used for firewood. He wept a little as he parted with it. A visitor, hearing the story of his gift, sent a beautiful red engine to Tonio in place of his piece of wood.

> Taken from *The Friday Miracle and other stories* ed Kaye Webb, published in aid of The Save the Children Fund, Penguin 1969, and used by permission.

Appendix 2: Suggested Songs and Hymns

Publishers of song/hymn books are given at end of list

Advent liturgy	Christmas is Coming, *Innkeepers and Light Sleepers,*
	The Holly and the Ivy, *Hymns and Psalms*
First Sunday of Advent	O come, O come Emmanuel, *Hymns and Psalms*
Second Sunday of Advent	Prepare ye the way of the Lord, *Godspell*
	The journey of life, *Come and Praise*
Third Sunday of Advent	There's a light upon the mountains, *Hymns and Psalms*
Fourth Sunday of Advent	Of the Father's love begotten, *Hymns and Psalms*
	Long ago prophets knew, *Hymns and Psalms*
	Let heaven and earth combine, *Hymns and Psalms*
Christmas Day	See amid the winter's snow, *Hymns and Psalms*
	Born in the night, *Hymns and Psalms*
	Amen Siakudumisa! *Many and Great*
First Sunday of Christmas	Hail to the Lord who comes, *Hymns and Psalms*
Second Sunday of Christmas	I am for you, *Wild Goose Songs Vol.1*
	(Heaven shall not wait)
Epiphany	The Servant King, *Let's Praise*
First Sunday in Ordinary Time	Be still, for the presence of the Lord, *Let's Praise*
	Spirit of God, unseen as the wind, *Common Ground*
Second Sunday in Ordinary Time	There is no moment of my life, *Hymns and Psalms*
	God be in my head, *Hymns and Psalms*
Third Sunday in Ordinary Time	Jesus came a-walking by the seashore, *Story Song*
Fourth Sunday in Ordinary Time	If I had a hammer, *Come and Praise*
Fifth Sunday in Ordinary Time	Every star shall sing a carol, *Partners in Praise*
Sixth Sunday in Ordinary Time	As if you were not there, *Love from Below*
	Inspired by love and anger, *Enemy of Apathy*
	God give us life, *Common Ground*
Seventh Sunday in Ordinary Time	We lay our broken world, *Common Ground*
Eighth Sunday in Ordinary Time	Jesu, lover of my soul, *Hymns and Psalms*
Sunday before Lent	Be still and know that I am God, *Enemy of Apathy*
First Sunday in Lent	Water of life, *Come and Praise*

Second Sunday in Lent	Lift high the cross, *Hymns and Psalms*
	Majesty, *Let's Praise*
	The royal banners forward go, *Hymns and Psalms*
	Kyrie Eleison (Russian), *Many and Great*
Third Sunday in Lent	Your words to me, *Hymns and Psalms*
Fourth Sunday in Lent	For God so loved the world, *Big Blue Planet*
	He came down that we may have love, *Big Blue Planet*
Fifth Sunday in Lent	O sacred head, sore wounded, *Hymns and Psalms*
Sixth Sunday in Lent	All glory, laud and honour, *Hymns and Psalms*
	Jesus, remember me, when you come into your kingdom, *Songs and Prayers from Taizé*
	When I survey, *Hymns and Psalms*
Easter Day	Halle, halle, halle, *Many and Great*
	Alleluia 2, *Come all you People*
	Alleluia, alleluia, *Sent by the Lord*
Second Sunday of Easter	The peace of the Lord, *Big Blue Planet*
	Alleluia, the Lord is risen (Appendix 1)
	Good Christians all, rejoice and sing, *Hymns and Psalms*
	The Peace of the Lord, *Big Blue Planet*
Third Sunday of Easter	Christ is alive, *Hymns and Psalms*
	Stand, O stand firm, *Many and Great*
Fourth Sunday of Easter	I lift my eyes, *Mission Praise*
	After darkness, light, *Hymns and Psalms*
Fifth Sunday of Easter	We shall be as one, *Songs of Fellowship*
	Christ is alive, let Christians sing, *Hymns and Psalms*
Sixth Sunday of Easter	Hevenu shalom, *Mission Praise*
	Ubi caritas, *Songs and Prayers from Taizé*
Seventh Sunday of Easter	Jesus Christ is waiting, *Enemy of Apathy*
Pentecost	Come down O love divine, *Hymns and Psalms*
	Wa wa wa Emimimo, *Many and Great*
	I will pour out my spirit, *Hymns and Psalms*
Trinity Sunday	Holy, holy, holy, *Hymns and Psalms*
	God has put a circle round us, *Big Blue Planet*
Ninth Sunday in Ordinary Time	Speak Lord in the stillness, *Mission Praise*
	Hushed was the evening hymn, *Hymns and Psalms*
Tenth Sunday in Ordinary Time	Come all you people, *Come all you People*
	Come Lord Jesus Come, *Big Blue Planet*
Eleventh Sunday in Ordinary Time	Just a Tiny Seed, *Big Blue Planet*
	Lord of creation, *Hymns and Psalms*

Twelfth Sunday in Ordinary Time	One day when we were fishing, *Big Blue Planet*
Thirteenth Sunday in Ordinary Time	Begone, unbelief, *Hymns and Psalms* All praise to our redeeming Lord, *Hymns and Psalms* Kum ba ya, *Hymns and Psalms*
Fourteenth Sunday in Ordinary Time	Domine deus, *Big Blue Planet* Kyrie, *Love from Below*
Fifteenth Sunday in Ordinary Time	It's a Happy Day , *Junior Praise* When you're feeling good, *Junior Praise 2* Jesus is my friend, *Big Blue Planet*
Sixteenth Sunday in Ordinary Time	Today I awake, *Common Ground* O Lord all the world belongs to you, *Come and Praise*
Seventeenth Sunday in Ordinary Time	Jesus the Lord said 'I am the bread', *Hymns and Psalms* There's a spirit in the air, *Hymns and Psalms* Bread is blessed and broken, *Common Ground*
Eighteenth Sunday in Ordinary Time	Come now, O Prince of Peace, *Common Ground* Brother, sister, let me serve you, *Common Ground*
Nineteenth Sunday in Ordinary Time	Come Holy Ghost, our souls inspire, *Hymns and Psalms*
Twentieth Sunday in Ordinary Time	Bread and fishes (Alan Bell), *Songs for Tomorrow* If you believe and I believe, *Sent by the Lord*
Twenty-first Sunday in Ordinary Time	The Lord is my light, *World Praise* St Patrick's breastplate (I bind unto myself this day), *Hymns and Psalms*
Twenty-second Sunday in Ordinary Time	Thuma mina, *Sent by the Lord*
Twenty-third Sunday in Ordinary Time	O for a thousand tongues to sing, *Hymns and Psalms*
Twenty-fourth Sunday in Ordinary Time	Stand, O stand firm, *Many and Great*
Twenty-fifth Sunday in Ordinary Time	He knew the greatness of the small, *Love from Below*
Twenty-sixth Sunday in Ordinary Time	Gloria, *Come all you People* O Lord, all the world belongs to you, *Let's Praise*
Twenty-seventh Sunday in Ordinary Time	Will you come and follow me, *Heaven shall not Wait*
Twenty-eighth Sunday in Ordinary Time	Can we by searching find out God? *Hymns and Psalms*

130

Twenty-ninth Sunday in Ordinary Time	When our confidence is shaken, *Hymns and Psalms*
Thirtieth Sunday in Ordinary Time	Christ's is the world, *Love from Below*
All Saints	For all the saints, *Hymns and Psalms*
Thirty-first Sunday in Ordinary Time	God the creator, *Love from Below*
Thirty-second Sunday in Ordinary Time	For your generous providing, *Common Ground*
Thirty-third Sunday in Ordinary Time	Behold, behold I make all things new, *Come all you People*
Sunday before Advent	Jesus shall reign where e'er the sun, *Hymns and Psalms*

Big Blue Planet, Stainer & Bell/Methodist Publishing House
Come all you People, Wild Goose Publications
Come and Praise, BBC Educational Publications
Common Ground, St Andrew's Press
Enemy of Apathy, Wild Goose Publications
Heaven shall not Wait, Wild Goose Publications
Hymns and Psalms, Methodist Publishing House
Innkeepers and Light Sleepers, Wild Goose Publications
Junior Praise, Marshall Pickering
Junior Praise 2, Marshall Pickering
Let's Praise, Marshall Pickering
Love from Below, Wild Goose Publications
Many and Great, Wild Goose Publications
Mission Praise, Marshall Pickering
Partners in Praise, Stainer & Bell/Chester House Publications
Sent by the Lord, Wild Goose Publications
Songs and Prayers from Taizé, Geoffrey Chapman/Mowbray
Songs of Fellowship, Kingsway
Story Song, Stainer & Bell/Methodist Publishing House
World Praise, Marshall Pickering

Index of Themes

Adoration, wonder, 36, 46, 53, 56, 58, 70, 86, 108
Advent, coming of Christ, 2, 4, 6, 8, 10, 118, 121
AIDS, 31
Anger, 30

Baptism, 39, 41, 88
Beginnings, 9, 15, 20, 51, 56, 72, 76, 90, 113
Bread (of life), 85, 87, 96
Breath of God, wind, spirit, 64, 65, 67, 91, 109
Brokenness, 28

Calling, 21, 22, 27, 83
Change, 65
Children of God, 104
Choices, 24, 30, 32
Cleansing, purification, 70, 94, 121
Collects, 10, 19, 34, 53, 55, 61, 68, 85, 117, 121
Commandments, 42, 114
Commitment, 17, 23. 24, 30, 35, 37, 40, 55, 59, 95, 114, 115
Community, 52, 54, 56, 68, 60, 62, 66, 92, 115
Conflict, 26
Cosmic child, 12
Covenant, 38, 42, 47
Creation, 12, 28, 56
Creativity of God, 4, 92
Cross, 41, 49, 82

Dance, 81
Death, 76, 113
Deliverance, 27, 51, 119, 121
Denial, 47
Desert, desolation *see* Wilderness
Discipleship, 22, 34, 37, 40, 67, 88, 98, 100
Diversity, difference, variety, 61, 110

Earth, renewal of , 91, 110
Evil, 26, 27, 109

CPSIA information can be obtained at www.ICGtesting.com
Printed in the USA
BVOW010105040213

312180BV00029B/392/P